The Ultimate Israeli Cookbook

111 Dishes From Israel To Cook Right Now

Slavka Bodic

Imprint: Independently published

Please sign up for free Balkan and Mediterranean recipes:
www.balkanfood.org

Introduction

Israeli cuisine has been globally known and coveted for its diverse flavors and aromas. In fact, its culinary culture has gained many influences from the entire Middle East, the centuries-old history of the region, and the unique Jewish traditions from this land. All those influences are specifically reflected through the diversity of meals that you'll find in the Israeli cuisine, whether you're enjoying entrees, sides, desserts, drinks or breakfasts. The great perk about Israeli food is that it's so rich and healthy due to the use of all nutritious ingredients like olives, dates, grains, legumes, and meat. I know a lot of people would love to try the exotic Israeli flavors and want to recreate the traditional recipes. So if you want the same, then look no further, as we're about to deliver a collection of 111 Israeli recipes in one place!

The Ultimate Israeli Cookbook will introduce you to Israeli cuisine and its culinary culture in a way that you must have never experienced before. It'll help you to explore a variety of Israeli recipes comprehensively. This cookbook is great for all those who are always keen to cook nutritious food and want to discover some unique flavors. With the help of this Israeli cuisine cookbook, you can create a complete Israeli menu at home, or you can try all the special Israeli recipes at your own festive celebrations.

In this cookbook, you'll find popular Israeli meals and the ones that you might not have heard of. From nourishing hummus dishes to all of the soups, desserts, drinks, main dishes, and salads, you can find them all in this amazing book. And all these Israeli recipes are created in such a simple way that those who aren't quite familiar with the Israeli culture, food, and language can still try and cook them at home with complete ease and convenience.

Plus, Israeli cuisine is full of flavorsome surprises that bring you a blend of eastern and western culinary traditions. So, if you want to add all those amazing meals to your menu, then give this book a thorough read, and you'll find all the right answers in one spot.

What you can uncover in this Cookbook:

1. An Overview About Israeli cuisine
2. Insights about Israel
3. Israeli breakfast recipes
4. Sides and appetizers
5. Main Dishes
6. Israeli desserts
7. Israeli Drinks

Let's try all these Israeli Recipes and recreate a complete menu to celebrate the amazing Israeli flavors and unique aromas.

Table Of Contents

Why Israeli Cuisine?

There are a lot of Israeli recipes that we normally have without even knowing their origins. The commonly enjoyed *baba ghanoush* and the *chickpea hummus* derive from this Middle Eastern region. Besides, there are several other meals that we are familiar with, and they all have Israeli origin. Though Israeli is a fairly new state, the region has a long and rather complicated history, which has left great influences on the people living there and their cultural and culinary preferences. The Israeli cuisine today reflects several different Middle Eastern influences and closely resembles the Syrian and Lebanese cuisine. On one hand, the cuisine also exhibits some of the Mediterranean influence because of the Jews who migrated from Europe and Mediterranean countries.

Though there are several styles of cooking, which had been and are still being used in Israeli cuisine presently, there are three popular styles that are mostly heard whenever a Jewish recipe is discussed. Why and how these styles differ from one another depends on the nature of the ingredients used and the origin of the recipes. We'll obtain a brief look at all those popular styles of Jewish food cooking.

First, the Ashkenazi Israeli food today is popularly known as the American Jewish cuisine. But the roots of the Ashkenazi food connect to Central and Eastern Europe. The traditions were later taken to America and then came to know as American. During the Middle Ages, when the Jews were expelled from Western Europe, they had to live in harsh conditions with limited ingredients in access. That time period deeply influenced the way they used to cook their food. Fewer components were added to the recipes. Consequently, those dishes weren't heavily spiced or not too flavorsome. Even today, people who only enjoy the mild tastes and lesser spicier variations opt for the Ashkenazic cuisine. In these recipes, only basic and mild spices are used to season the meats and vegetables.

Then comes the Sephardic cuisine, which you might have heard of, since it's the most popular of all. The cuisine is named for its connection with the Sephardic Jews living in Portugal, Span, and Iberia. When these Jews traveled to other parts of the world, their culinary traditions also disseminated with them. Soon the Sephardic Jews inhabited the areas around the Mediterranean Sea like Greece, Turkey, Balkans, Arab countries, and North Africa. The use of heavy spices, condiments, herbs, and other rich ingredients are common in this cuisine. Since it was influenced by the local cuisine of all those regions, it further adopted the diversity of ingredients in various ways. Shabbat and Passover holiday dishes particularly belong to this type of Israeli cuisine.

Next, Mizrahi is another subtype of Israeli cuisine that takes all the culinary traditions from Jews living in the Middle East, North Africa, Asia, and Arab countries. It's also known as the oriental Jewish recipe due to the nature of its origin. This cuisine depends mostly on the fresh ingredients like the fresh meat is soaked and salted through the process of *shechita* before using.

Israel

Israel is a Middle Eastern state located on the shore of the Mediterranean Sea and the Red Sea. It shares its land borders with Lebanon, Syria, Jordan, the Palestinian territories, and Egypt. The country is known for its rich history and dramatic evolution over the years. It's also the religious center of all the Jews around the world. The region is inhabited by people of different origins. There are a lot of ancient heritage sites that are worth visiting in the country. There are number of old churches and synagogues to explore. The Great Synagogue in the capital Tel Aviv is a sensational sight to see. Then you can go kayaking in the Jordan River. The Golan Jeep Safari tour was also a fun experience for me. For every adventure and fun lover, there are several other exciting adventures waiting in this memorable country.

We can't really trace the history of the Israeli culinary traditions as they are many as three thousand years old. Over the years, those traditions evolved under the ethnic influences in Asia, Europe, and Africa. Still, the recipes which are today enjoyed links to the ancient kings of Israel dating baking to the era of 968 BCE. Then in Roman and Hellenistic culture, it became heavily influenced by the traditions of the period prevalent among the aristocracy and the priests. Lavish meals used to be served, including fish, alcoholic drinks, vegetables, pickles, meat, olives, beef, tarts, and fruits. As of today, many of the ingredients used and served during those ages are still being employed in modern-day Israeli cuisine, like figs, olives, dates, wheat, grapes, pomegranates, barley, etc. Locally grown products are most widely applied in this cuisine, and people love to consume their own produce. But with modernization, they also turned towards exotic spices and started to use them continually.

All in all, geography exerted the most influence on the cuisine over the course of years; the availability of certain ingredients in a region added peculiar flavors to their respective recipes. For instance, Mediterranean Jewish cuisine makes the best use of vegetables, fruits, fish, and dairy products. Those from the Middle East or Persian origins use more of the spices and rich flavors. Israeli recipes are known for their unique style of cooking. They all demand special techniques and styles to add aromas and flavors to the ordinary ingredients. That may include cooking on slow heat for a long time, pickling with spices, or using aromatic spices like saffron to infuse more flavors. One thing for when it comes to Jewish cuisine is that the food always guarantees the best taste with loads of aromas!

Besides, we all know that when Jewish holidays are marked on the calendars, we instantly start imagining all the flavors they bring along with them. The cuisine has a lot to offer for special festive occasions, like there's plenty of food cooked for Shabbat, including gefilte fish, Jachnun, challah, Sufganiyot, hamin, malawach, and me orav yerushalmi. If you aren't familiar with these names, then hang on, as we'll be shortly sharing all these recipes in the sections to come. These recipes don't require hard labor; you can easily prepare to fit your health needs by substituting the ingredients with healthy ones.

Breakfast

Eggplant And Walnut Frittata

Preparation time: 10 minutes
Cook time: 32 minutes
Nutrition facts (per serving): 254 cal (14g fat, 25g protein, 4g fiber)

The eggplant walnut frittata is a perfect breakfast meal, filled with the richness of eggplants and barberries. Serve warm with freshly toasted bread.

Ingredients (4 servings)

2 cups walnuts, chopped
1 large eggplant, peeled and coarsely chopped
2 medium red onions, coarsely chopped
1 heaping teaspoon freshly ground black pepper
¾ teaspoon kosher salt
6 large eggs, beaten
½ cup dried red Persian barberries
2 ½ tablespoon unsalted butter

Preparation

Let your oven preheat at 375 degrees F and place its rack in the top third portion. Add 1 ¾ cup of walnuts to a food processor and grind to get fine crumbs. Transfer it to a plate and add the onion and eggplant to the processor. Finely mince them in the processor. Place and spread this mixture in a fine sieve and place a small plate over it. Leave it for about 10 minutes to release all the water. Toss this mixture with salt and pepper in a bowl. Add the walnut ground, eggs, and barberries. Now melt butter in a skillet, place over medium heat. Add egg mixture and cook for 2 minutes until it is set. Place this pan in the oven and bake for 30 minutes until it turns golden brown from the top. Allow it to cool, and then transfer to a platter. Garnish with pomegranate seeds, barberries, and walnuts. Enjoy.

Malabi (Milk Pudding)

Preparation time: 15 minutes

Cook time: 5 minutes

Nutrition facts (per serving): 352 cal (15g fat, 24g protein, 4g fiber)

This Israeli milk pudding is one healthy breakfast dish that can be served with pomegranate toppings. It's best topped with fresh fruits.

Ingredients (8 servings)

Crust

1 cup roasted pistachios

¼ cup of sugar

A pinch of salt

3 tablespoons coconut oil

Malabi

2 can (13 ½ ounces) full-fat coconut milk

6 tablespoons cornstarch

1 tablespoon vanilla bean paste

1 teaspoon rose water

¼ teaspoon salt

½ cup of sugar

Persimmons

1 cup Fuyu persimmon, chopped

1 teaspoon vanilla bean paste

1 tablespoon lemon zest

1 teaspoon sugar

Pomegranate arils

Preparation

Crush the pistachios with salt, coconut oil, and sugar in a food processor. Divide the pistachios into 8 small serving glasses. Mix ½ cup coconut milk with vanilla paste, rose water, and cornstarch in a bowl. Mix the remaining coconut milk with sugar and salt in a saucepan and warm it up over medium heat. Stir in the cornstarch mixture and cook for 2 minutes with constant stirring. Divide this mixture into the serving glasses and allow them to cool. Cover and refrigerate for 4 hours. Meanwhile, mix persimmon with lemon zest, sugar, and vanilla in a bowl. Divide this mixture over the refrigerated Malabi. Garnish with pomegranate arils. Serve.

Baked Salmon Croquettes

Preparation time: 5 minutes
Cook time: 12 minutes
Nutrition facts (per serving): 205 cal (11.8g fat, 10g protein, 2g fiber)

These salmon croquettes are typical Israeli breakfast patties, a must on the Israeli menu. It has this rich mix of salmon with carrots and matzo meal that I love.

Ingredients (6 servings)
1-pound salmon, cooked
2 large carrots, peeled, diced, and roasted
½ cup ground matzo meal
¼ cup parsley, chopped
2 tablespoons mustard
2 eggs
½ cup onion, diced
2 garlic cloves, minced
Salt and black pepper to taste
Olive oil
Red pepper flakes

Preparation
At 425 degrees F, preheat your oven. Sauté the garlic and onions with oil in a skillet until soft. Transfer this mixture to a bowl. Stir in the herbs, matzo meal, egg, roasted carrots, salmon, mustard, black pepper, and salt, then mix well. Make small flat patties from this mixture and place them into a baking sheet greased with olive oil. Bake them for 6 minutes per side. Serve warm.

Whole-Wheat Pita Bread

Preparation time: 15 minutes
Cook time: 28 minutes
Nutrition facts (per serving): 386 cal (3g fat, 24g protein, 5g fiber)

You won't know until you try it! That's what people told me about this pita bread, and it indeed tasted more unique and flavorsome than other breads I've tried.

Ingredients (4 servings)

3 cups lukewarm water
½ cup honey
1 ½ tablespoons salt
1 ½ tablespoon granulated yeast
½ cup olive oil
¼ cup vital wheat gluten
4 cups whole wheat flour
3 ½ cups all-purpose flour

Preparation

Mix water with salt and honey in a bowl and stir in the olive oil and yeast. Stir in the flours and mix well until it makes smooth dough. Cover the prepared dough and leave it for 3 hours. At 500 degrees F, preheat your oven. Place a suitable baking stone in the oven while preheating. Divide the prepared dough into four equal-sized pieces and spread each portion into ⅛-inch-thick rounds. Place one round on the baking stone and bake for 7 minutes. Cook the remaining pita rounds in the same manner. Serve warm.

Broccoli Kugel

Preparation time: 5 minutes

Cook time: 1 hour 15 minutes

Nutrition facts (per serving): 520 cal (32g fat, 43g protein, 0g fiber)

Simple and easy to make, this recipe is a staple on this menu. Broccoli kugel is a delight for the breakfast table.

Ingredients (6 servings)

1 (2-pound) bag frozen broccoli, chopped

1 cup light mayonnaise

4 eggs

1 ½ teaspoons salt

¼ teaspoon black pepper

1 pinch cayenne pepper

Preparation

At 375 degrees F, preheat your oven. Grease a suitable 9-inch baking dish with cooking spray. Mix broccoli with cayenne peppers, black pepper, salt, eggs, and mayonnaise in a bowl. Spread this mixture in the baking dish and bake for 1 hour and 15 minutes. Serve warm.

Potato Kugel

Preparation time: 5 minutes

Cook time: 60 minutes

Nutrition facts (per serving): 445 cal (21g fat, 60g protein, 4g fiber)

Potato Kugel is one of the traditional Israeli breakfast dishes made with onions, potatoes, eggs, and zucchini that you can enjoy with toasted bread.

Ingredients (6 servings)

2 Spanish onions, grated

6 potatoes, grated

1 parsnip, grated

1 zucchini, grated

6 eggs

1 ½ tablespoons salt

½ teaspoon black pepper

⅓ cup oil

Preparation

At 350 degrees F, preheat your oven. Grease a 9x13 inches baking pan with oil. Beat the eggs with black pepper and salt in a bowl. Stir in zucchini, parsnip, potatoes, and onions. Spread the potato mixture in a pan and bake for 1 hour. Slice and serve warm.

Zaatar Flatbread

Preparation time: 15 minutes
Cook time: 20 minutes
Nutrition facts (per serving): 256 cal (5.2g fat, 3g protein, 18g fiber)

Have you tried Zaatar flatbread for breakfast? Well, here's an Israeli delight that adds the exotic Zaatar flavor to your morning meal in a delicious way.

Ingredients (4 servings)

1 (¼-ounce) packet active dry yeast
¾ cup of warm water
½ cup olive oil
1 cup whole-wheat flour
1 cup all-purpose flour
1 teaspoon salt
¼ cup Za'atar
2 tablespoons white and black sesame blend

Preparation

Mix the warm water with yeast in the bowl of a stand mixer and leave it for 10 minutes. Stir in ¼ cup oil, flour, and ½ teaspoon salt. Mix well, add flour, and stir until it makes smooth dough. Knead this dough for 8 minutes using a dough hook. Transfer the prepared dough to a suitable greased bowl and cover it with a plastic sheet.

Leave this dough for 1 ½ hour. Grease a baking sheet with oil. At 375 degrees F, preheat your oven. Spread the prepared dough on the baking sheet into a 10x12 inch rectangle. Poke the prepared dough with your finger, brush it with olive oil, and drizzle Za'atar and salt on top. Leave the prepared dough for 30 minutes and then bake it for 20 minutes, then serve warm.

Baked Portobello Shakshuka

Preparation time: 10 minutes
Cook time: 28 minutes
Nutrition facts (per serving): 478 cal (16g fat, 14g protein, 2g fiber)

This baked Portobello shakshuka tastes heavenly when cooked and baked at home. Serve warm with your favorite toppings and bread on the side.

Ingredients (8 servings)
1 bag baby spinach
1 tablespoon olive oil
2 (8 ounces) containers matbucha (traditional dip)
8 Portobello mushrooms see instructions
8 eggs
Salt and black pepper to taste

Preparation
At 400 degrees F, preheat your oven. Destem the mushrooms and spread them on a baking sheet. Drizzle black pepper, salt, and olive oil over the mushrooms. Bake for 10 minutes. Sauté the spinach with olive oil, black pepper, and salt in a baking pan until wilted. Add the matbucha. Divide the spinach mixture to the mushrooms and crack one egg into each mushroom. Bake them again for 18 minutes. Serve warm.

Shakshuka With Haloumi Cheese

Preparation time: 15 minutes
Cook time: 2 hours 5 minutes
Nutrition facts (per serving): 256 cal (16g fat, 9g protein, 6g fiber)

Shakshuka with halloumi cheese is another nutritious yet simple meal for the breakfast table. It has adds lots of nutrients and fibers, along with healthy ingredients that are cooked together in a tempting combination.

Ingredients (6 servings)

2 (28-ounce) cans whole peeled tomatoes, drained
4 garlic cloves, chopped
1 green bell pepper, roasted and chopped
2 tablespoons olive oil
1 tablespoon paprika
6 eggs
½ cup halloumi cheese slices, crumbled
Scallions, chopped
Salt to taste

Preparation

Strain the tomatoes and transfer them to a cooking pot. Crush the tomatoes and add olive oil, salt, roasted peppers, paprika, and garlic. Next, cook for 2 hours on medium heat. Make small-sized wells in the mixture and crack one egg into each well. Cover and cook for 5 minutes on low heat. Garnish with cheese and scallions. Serve warm.

Spinach Shakshuka

Preparation time: 15 minutes
Cook time: 15 minutes
Nutrition facts (per serving): 410 cal (6g fat, 10g protein, 1.4g fiber)

Try this spinach shakshuka for your breakfast, and you'll forget about the rest. The recipe is simple and gives you loads of nutrients in one place.

Ingredients (6 servings)
¼ cup of olive oil
1 medium onion, diced
1 small hot pepper, diced
5 garlic cloves, chopped
3 tablespoon coriander, diced
3 tablespoon parsley, diced
½ teaspoon salt
¼ teaspoons black pepper
12 ounces fresh spinach, chopped
1 tablespoon fresh lemon juice
6 large eggs
¼ cup of Feta cheese, crumbled

Preparation
Sauté the onion and hot pepper with oil in a pan until soft. Stir in the black pepper, salt, herbs, and garlic, and then cook for 3 minutes. Add lemon juice and spinach and then cover to cook on low heat for 7 minutes. Spread the mixture in the pan. Make a small well in this mixture and crack one egg into each. Cover and cook for 5 minutes. Garnish with cheese. Serve.

Labneh

Preparation time: 10 minutes
Nutrition facts (per serving): 591 cal (33g fat, 9g protein, 2g fiber)

Labneh is known as the classic Israeli breakfast, which is a light yogurt meal. It's super easy and simple to make at home.

Ingredients (4 servings)
Olive oil
1-quart Greek yogurt
1 teaspoon salt

Preparation
Mix the yogurt with salt in a bowl. Place a suitable cheesecloth in a strainer and pour the yogurt into the cheesecloth. Loosely cover it with a plastic sheet and refrigerate it overnight. Transfer the yogurt to a bowl and drizzle Za'atar and olive oil on top. Serve.

Israeli Breakfast Sandwich (Sabich)

Preparation time: 15 minutes
Cook time: 47 minutes
Nutrition facts (per serving): 226 cal (2.4g fat, 4g protein, 1g fiber)

Sabich is one of the Israeli specialties, so everyone must try this interesting fusion of eggplant and salad filling.

Ingredients (4 servings)
1 large eggplant, sliced
3 tablespoons olive oil
Salt and black pepper, to taste
4 large eggs

Israeli Salad
4 whole-wheat pitas, warmed
1 cup prepared hummus
1 cup red cabbage, shredded
2 plum tomatoes, seeded and diced
1 small English cucumber, diced
3 tablespoons parsley, chopped
Juice of 1 lemon
2 tablespoons olive oil
1 tablespoon red wine vinegar
Salt and black pepper, to taste

Preparation

Prepare the salad by mixing its ingredients in a bowl. At 400 degrees F, preheat your oven. Coat the eggplant slices with black pepper, salt, and olive oil. Place the slices on a baking sheet and bake for 30 minutes. Boil eggs in a pot filled with water for 17 minutes, then drain. Transfer the eggs to cold water, drain and peel. Cut the eggs into slices. Open each pita bread piece into a pocket and add ¼ cup hummus, eggplant slices, Israeli salad, hot sauce, and cabbage.

Israeli Breakfast Salad

Preparation time: 15 minutes
Nutrition facts (per serving): 471 cal (17g fat, 16g protein, 0.7g fiber)

This breakfast salad is the best way to enjoy fresh vegetables in the morning in a savory style. Made from cucumber, onion, and cheese, it's truly a delight to serve at your breakfast.

Ingredients (4 servings)

2 cucumbers, peeled
½ cup cottage cheese
½ cup feta cheese, crumbled
¼ cup onion, grated and drained
1 green pepper, seeded and chopped
¼ cup lemon juice
¼ cup olive oil
Salt and black pepper, to taste
1 sprig of fresh mint, garnish

Preparation

Place the cucumber in a colander, drizzle salt on top, and leave it for 30 minutes. Dice the cucumbers and transfer them to a bowl. Add olive oil, lemon juice, green pepper, onion, black pepper, salt, and cheese. Mix well. Garnish with mint sprigs. Serve.

Challah

Preparation time: 10 minutes
Cook time: 30 minutes
Nutrition facts (per serving): 317 cal (14g fat, 8.9g protein, 0.3g fiber)

The famous challah bread is here to complete your breakfast menu. Now you can make a large challah loaf using this simple recipe.

Ingredients (12 servings)
Dough
1 2/3 cup water

3 tablespoons 2 teaspoons yeast

5 cups all-purpose flour

2 cups whole wheat flour

2 eggs

½ cup of sugar

1 tablespoon salt

5 tablespoons sunflower oil

Egg wash
1 large egg

1 tablespoon water

1 pinch salt

Preparation
Attach and fix a dough hook to a stand mixer and mix the yeast with water in the mixer bowl. Leave it for 5 minutes. Stir in the sugar, oil, salt, eggs, and flour. Mix well until it makes smooth dough. Knead this prepared dough on a floured

surface for 4 minutes. Transfer the prepared dough to a suitable greased bowl, cover, and leave it for 2 hours. At 350 degrees F, preheat your oven. Grease a baking sheet with parchment paper. Divide the prepared dough into three equal-sized portions. Roll each portion into three ropes and pinch the three ropes together at one end. Braid the three dough ropes and place them on a baking sheet. Leave the prepared dough for 30 minutes and then bake the bread for 30 minutes.

Israeli Tahini Toast

Preparation time: 15 minutes
Cook time: 10 minutes
Nutrition facts (per serving): 971 cal (66g fat, 32g protein, 3g fiber)

If you haven't tried the Israeli tahini taste before, then here comes a simple and easy to cook recipe that you can prepare at home in no time with minimum efforts.

Ingredients (2 servings)

2 pieces of bread, toasted
⅓ green pepper, diced
⅓ yellow pepper, diced
5 grape tomatoes, sliced
2 tablespoons parsley, chopped
1½ teaspoons Lemon juice
Pinch of Salt

Tahini sauce

½ cup tahini
¼ cup of water
2 tablespoons lemon juice
1 pinch of salt

Preparation

Heat a greased skillet and toast the bread slices until golden brown. Mix the bell peppers with tomatoes, lemon juice, parsley, and salt in a bowl. Prepare the tahini sauce by stirring its ingredients in a bowl. Spread the tahini sauce over the toasts and top them with a vegetable mixture. Serve.

Appetizers and Sides

Baba Ghanoush with Tahini

Preparation time: 5 minutes
Nutrition facts (per serving): 231 cal (20g fat, 22g protein, 6g fiber)

Baba ghanoush prepared with tahini is one of the most delicious appetizers or side meals to try in this cuisine. You can try it with different variations for its toppings.

Ingredients (8 servings)

2 medium eggplants
½ cup pure tahini
½ cup yogurt
Juice of 1 lemon
2 garlic cloves, chopped
Salt, to taste
Chopped parsley and mint
Olive oil

Preparation

Set a grill on medium heat and grill the eggplants until charred. Slice the eggplants and transfer them to a colander placed in a bowl. Leave them for 5 minutes to drain the liquid and reserve the liquid. Peel and deseed the eggplants and then transfer the pulp to a food processor. Add lemon juice, salt, garlic, tahini, and yogurt and blend well until smooth. Stir in the mint, parsley, and olive oil. Mix well and serve.

Matbucha

Preparation time: 10 minutes
Cook time: 20 minutes
Nutrition facts (per serving): 135 cal (10g fat, 2.4g protein, 2g fiber)

Count on this matbucha to make your dinner extra special and surprise your loved one with the ultimate flavors.

Ingredients (8 servings)

¼ cup olive oil

3 garlic cloves, minced

5 tomatoes, chopped

5 green bell peppers, chopped

1 jalapeno pepper, chopped

1 teaspoon paprika

1 teaspoon black pepper

1 pinch sea salt

1 lemon, juiced

Preparation

Sauté the jalapeno pepper, bell pepper, tomatoes, garlic with olive oil, salt, and black pepper in a large pot for 20 minutes on high heat. Reduce the heat, then cover to cook for 2 hours. Add lemon juice then mix well. Serve.

Potato Latkes

Preparation time: 10 minutes
Cook time: 20 minutes
Nutrition facts (per serving): 289 cal (13g fat, 6.8g protein, 3g fiber)

These potato latkes will melt your heart away with their great flavors. The latkes are super crispy on the outside and taste best with tomato sauce or yogurt dip.

Ingredients (5 servings)
4 potatoes, peeled and cubed
1 onion, chopped
2 eggs
2 teaspoons salt
2 tablespoons all-purpose flour
1 teaspoon baking powder
¼ cup canola oil

Preparation
Mix the baking powder, flour, salt, eggs, onion, and ¼ potatoes in a food processor. Blend until finely chopped. Next, add the remaining potatoes and pulse to chop again. Scoop out ⅓ cup of the potatoes mixture at a time to make one latke. Add canola oil in a skillet and heat over medium heat. Fry the latke in the hot oil for 3 minutes per side until golden brown. Serve warm.

Cheese Bourekas

Preparation time: 15 minutes
Cook time: 30 minutes
Nutrition facts (per serving): 294 cal (9g fat, 20g protein, 0.7g fiber)

If you haven't tried the cheese bourekas before, then here's a delectable recipe that you can recreate at home easily.

Ingredients (12 servings)

2 eggs

2 cups mozzarella cheese, shredded

1 teaspoon dried parsley

1 pinch garlic powder

1 pinch onion powder

1 pinch salt

1 pinch black pepper

1 (17 ½ ounce) package of frozen puff pastry

2 teaspoons water

2 tablespoons sesame seeds

Preparation

At 350 degrees F, preheat your oven. Grease a baking sheet with cooking spray. Beat 1 egg with cheese, salt, black pepper, onion powder, garlic powder, and parsley in a bowl. Spread the ready-made puff pastry sheets on a floured surface cut each into six squares. Beat the remaining egg with 2 teaspoon water in a bow. Divide the cheese mixture onto the center of each pastry square and fold the pastry around the filling into a triangle. Next, pinch the edges to seal the filling. Brush the pastry with the egg wash and place them on the baking sheet. Lastly, drizzle sesame seeds on top. Bake them for almost 30 minutes until golden brown and then serve warm.

Colorful Tahini

Preparation time: 15 minutes
Cook time: 1 hour 30 minutes
Nutrition facts (per serving): 230 cal (4.2g fat, 10g protein, 1.4g fiber)

If you love to adorn your snack table with lots of colors, then this combination of tahini is best for you. Serve them separately or prepare a mixed platter.

Ingredients (8 servings)

Acorn Squash Tahini
2 medium acorn squash
¼ cup tahini
Freshly squeezed lemon juice
¼ teaspoon salt
Crushed ginger

Beet Tahini
2 medium beets
½ cup tahini
1 teaspoon lemon juice
½ teaspoon salt

Spinach Tahini
1-pound spinach
Olive oil
¼ cup tahini
½ teaspoon lemon juice
½ teaspoon salt

Preparation

At 300 degrees F, preheat your oven. Slice the acorn squash in half and deseed it. Place them on a baking sheet and roast the acorn for 45 minutes until soft. Peel off the squash's skin and mash the flesh in a bowl. Stir in the tahini, salt, ginger, and lemon juice and mix well. Wrap the beets in foil and place them on a baking sheet and bake at 480 degrees F for 30-40 minutes until soft. Peel the roasted beets and pulse in a blender until smooth. Add the salt, lemon juice, and tahini, and then mix well. Sauté the spinach with olive oil in a saucepan for 5 minutes. Next, transfer to a colander to drain all the liquid. Add the drained spinach to a food processor and add salt, lemon juice, and tahini, and then blend until smooth. Divide the three tahinis into serving bowls. Serve.

Sambusaks with Chickpeas

Preparation time: 10 minutes
Cook time: 20 minutes
Nutrition facts (per serving): 253 cal (14g fat, 10g protein, 2g fiber)

Here's another classic recipe for your snack and appetizer collection. Serve it with a tangy sauce and enjoy the best of it.

Ingredients (11 servings)

1 ½ cups all-purpose flour
1 tablespoon cornstarch
½ teaspoon salt
1 teaspoon baking powder
3 tablespoons vegetable oil
⅓ cup of warm water
1 onion, chopped
1 teaspoon vegetable oil
1 (15 ounces) can garbanzo beans, mashed
¼ bunch fresh cilantro, chopped
1 teaspoon ground cumin
1 teaspoon ground coriander
Salt and black pepper to taste
2 cups vegetable oil for frying
11 eggs

Preparation

Mix 3 tablespoons of oil with water, baking powder, salt, cornstarch, and flour in a bowl until it makes dough. Cover and leave the prepared dough for about

10 minutes. Divide the prepared dough into 10 portions and spread each dough piece on a floured surface into a 5 inches circle. Sauté the onion with 1 teaspoon oil in a skillet for 10 minutes until brown. Stir in black pepper, salt, coriander, cumin, cilantro, and garbanzo beans. Add 2 cups oil to a deep skillet and heat to 350 degrees F. Crack an egg in a ramekin and cover it with wax paper. Cook the egg for 40 seconds in the microwave on high heat. Divide the bean filling at the center of the prepared dough circles and divide the egg on top. Fold the circles in half and crimp their edges with a fork. Deep fry the beans sambusaks in hot oil for 3 minutes per side until golden brown. Serve warm.

Zucchini Baba Ghanoush

Preparation time: 10 minutes
Cook time: 15 minutes
Nutrition facts (per serving): 162 cal (13g fat, 7.5g protein, 2g fiber)

If you can't think of anything to cook and make in a short time, then try this zucchini baba ghanoush recipe because it offers great taste to serve at the table.

Ingredients (6 servings)

2 large zucchinis, halved
2 tablespoons olive oil
½ tablespoon salt
1 small garlic clove
1 lemon, juiced
½ cup tahini
¼ cup water

Preparation

At 450 degrees F, preheat your oven. Toss the zucchini halves with 1 tablespoon olive oil and salt in a bowl. Spread the zucchinis on a baking sheet and bake for 15 minutes, then allow them to cool. Chop the zucchinis and add them to a blender. Add the olive oil, salt, garlic, lemon juice, tahini, and water. Finally, blend until smooth. Serve.

Edamame Hummus

Preparation time: 15 minutes
Nutrition facts (per serving): 106 cal (9g fat, 4g protein, 0.1g fiber)

The appetizing edamame hummus makes a great addition to the menu, and they look great when served at the table.

Ingredients (6 servings)

2 cups edamame, shelled and cooked
¼ cup oil
3 tablespoons lemon juice
2 teaspoons garlic, chopped
¾ teaspoon cumin, ground
½ teaspoon salt

Preparation

Add the edamame, salt, cumin, garlic, and lemon juice to a food processor. Lastly, blend until smooth. Serve.

Pinto Bean Hummus

Preparation time: 15 minutes
Nutrition facts (per serving): 79 cal (5.2g fat, 2.8g protein, 3g fiber)

If you haven't tried this pinto bean hummus, then you must now as it has no parallel in taste and texture.

Ingredients (8 servings)

2 cups Pinto beans, cooked
1 cup scallion, sliced
1 tablespoon roasted garlic puree
¼ cup mint leaves, sliced
¼ cup tahini
¼ teaspoon black pepper
⅛ teaspoon cayenne pepper
2 tablespoons lemon juice

Pinto Mint Relish

1 cup cooked pinto beans, drained
¼ cup scallion, sliced
½ cup feta cheese, crumbled
2 tablespoons olive oil
⅛ teaspoon crushed red pepper flakes
1 tablespoon lemon juice
1 tablespoon sliced mint leaves

Cayenne pepper for garnish
Olive oil for garnish

Preparation

Blend the pinto beans with garlic and scallion in a blender until smooth. Add lemon juice, cayenne, salt, black pepper, tahini, and mint, and then mix well for 1 minute. Prepare the relish by stirring 1 cup pinto beans with red pepper, mint, lemon juice, olive oil, feta cheese, and green onion in a bowl. Serve the hummus with the relish on top. Serve.

Green Peas Hummus

Preparation time: 10 minutes
Nutrition facts (per serving): 231 cal (9.5g fat, 9.7g protein, 9g fiber)

Who doesn't like to have more green? Green peas lovers will love this green pea hummus on the menu.

Ingredients (8 servings)
3 cups frozen peas, thawed
¼ cup tahini
1 garlic clove, chopped
2 tablespoons tamari
2 tablespoons water
1 sheet nori, shredded
1 tablespoon white sesame seeds

Preparation
Blend the peas with tahini, garlic, tamari, water, and half of the nori shreds in a food processor until pureed. Garnish with sesame seeds and remaining nori. Serve.

Walnut Hummus

Preparation time: 15 minutes
Nutrition facts (per serving): 232 cal (11g fat, 13g protein, 3g fiber)

Try this no-cook walnut hummus and serve it with crispy crackers and chips. It takes about just a few minutes to prepare and serve it.

Ingredients (8 servings)
½ cup California walnuts, toasted
1 can (19 ounces) chickpeas, drained and rinsed
¼ cup Italian salad dressing
½ teaspoon cayenne pepper

Preparation
Add the walnuts, chickpeas, Italian salad dressing, and cayenne pepper to a blender and pulse until smooth. Serve.

Lavash Nachos

Preparation time: 15 minutes
Cook time: 10 minutes
Nutrition facts (per serving): 196 cal (3g fat, 12g protein, 3g fiber)

Lavash nachos are another Israeli-inspired delight that you should definitely try on this cuisine. Serve with a flavorsome sauce.

Ingredients (8 servings)
Nonstick vegetable oil spray
4 lavash sheets, cut into 2-inch triangles
1 can of cannellini beans, drained and rinsed
1 large white onion, chopped
4 ounces shredded mozzarella

Preparation
At 350 degrees F, preheat your oven. Spread the lavash triangles on a baking sheet, mist them with cooking spray, and bake for 5 minutes. Top the chips with shredded cheese, onions, and beans and bake for 5 minutes. Serve with mashed avocados. Serve.

Falafel

Preparation time: 10 minutes
Cook time: 12 minutes
Nutrition facts (per serving): 343 cal (13g fat, 15g protein, 2g fiber)

Falafels are a must to have on every Middle Eastern menu. This chickpea falafels recipe will yield crispy and soft falafels.

Ingredients (6 servings)

2 cups dried chickpeas, soaked overnight
Canola oil for deep frying
1 medium yellow onion, chopped
3 garlic cloves, chopped
1 tablespoon coriander seeds
1 cup pitted Kalamata olive
1 ½ teaspoons salt
½ teaspoon ground cumin
½ teaspoon black pepper

Preparation

Drain the soaked chickpeas and transfer to a bowl. Chop the garlic and onion in a food processor, t add the coriander seeds, chickpeas, and the rest of the ingredients to blend well. Bake 1 ½ inch balls from this mixture and keep them aside. Preheat oil in a deep-frying pan to 350 degrees F and deep fry the falafel balls for 3 minutes until brown. Serve.

Tahini Sesame Kale Chips

Preparation time: 10 minutes
Cook time: 10 minutes
Nutrition facts (per serving): 101 cal (3g fat, 14g protein, 4g fiber)

How about the delicious Tahini sesame kale chips? If you haven't tried them before, now is the time to cook this delicious delight at home using simple and healthy ingredients.

Ingredients (4 servings)

1 bunch kale
Juice from 2 limes
2 tablespoon olive oil
4 tablespoon tahini
1 teaspoon crushed red pepper flakes
⅛ teaspoon salt
⅛ teaspoon black pepper
1 tablespoon sesame seeds

Preparation

At 375 degrees F, preheat your oven. Toss the kale with the remaining ingredients on a baking sheet and roast them for 10 minutes. Serve.

Salads

Potato Salad

Preparation time: 10 minutes
Cook time: 20 minutes
Nutrition facts (per serving): 424 cal (29g fat, 12g protein, 6g fiber)

Try making the delicious potato salad with a delicious combination of boiled potatoes and mayonnaise at home to enjoy the best of the Israeli flavors!

Ingredients (6 servings)

2 pounds russet potatoes, peeled
¾ cup mayonnaise
1 cup frozen peas and carrots
6 hard-boiled eggs, chopped
6 Israeli pickles, chopped
½ cup spicy mustard
Salt and black pepper, to taste

Preparation

Add the potatoes to a pot filled with salted water and cook for 20 minutes on a simmer until soft. Drain and transfer the potatoes to a colander. Chop the eggs and pickles and then transfer to a salad bowl. Dice the potatoes and add to the bowl. Stir in the carrots, peas, mustard, mayonnaise, salt, and black pepper. Mix well and serve.

Couscous and Cranberry Salad

Preparation time: 15 minutes
Nutrition facts (per serving): 423 cal (6g fat, 38g protein, 0g fiber)

The couscous and cranberry salad goes perfectly with all the Israeli entrees. This recipe will add a lot of appeal and color to your dinner table.

Ingredients (4 servings)

½ cup dried cranberries
1 teaspoon ground cinnamon
¼ teaspoon ground cumin
1 cup cooked couscous
¼ cup vegetable oil
2 tablespoons rice vinegar
⅓ cup sliced almonds, toasted
⅓ cup green onion, chopped
2 tablespoons chopped fresh mint

Preparation

Mix the couscous with all the dressing and salad ingredients in a salad bowl and serve.

Bulgur Salad

Preparation time: 15 minutes
Cook time: 25 minutes
Nutrition facts (per serving): 378 cal (11g fat, 33g protein, 1.2g fiber)

The Israeli bulgur salad is here to complete your Israeli menu. Its fiber-rich content makes it super healthy and nutritious.

Ingredients (4 servings)
¾ cup bulgur wheat, dry
1 cup lentils, rinsed and drained
2 tablespoons garlic olive oil
1 cup green onions, sliced
1 red pepper, cut into squares
3 cups spinach leaves, cut into strips
2 teaspoons dried dill weed
8 ounces yogurt
½ cup almonds, toasted and sliced
Salt and black pepper to taste

Preparation
At 350 degrees F, preheat your oven. Spread the sliced almonds on a dry baking sheet and roast them for 10 minutes. Boil the bulgur in 2 cups of boiling water in a saucepan for 20 minutes and then drain. Sauté the onion with the pepper squares in a pan for 5 minutes. Stir in the bulgur and lentils and then mix well. Transfer to a salad bowl and stir in all remaining ingredients. Mix well and serve.

Israeli Leafy Green Salad

Preparation time: 10 minutes
Nutrition facts (per serving): 392 cal (19g fat, 25g protein, 2g fiber)

The leafy green salad is here to add flavors to your dinner table, but this time with a mix of cucumber and lettuce.

Ingredients (4 servings)
Salad
1 cucumber, diced
2 medium tomatoes, diced
1 head of romaine lettuce, shredded
2 scallions, chopped or ½ red onion diced
2 tablespoons chopped parsley

Dressing
2 tablespoons lemon juice
1 tablespoon olive oil
2 teaspoons white wine vinegar
1 dash of salt
1 dash of black pepper

Preparation
Add and toss all the vinegar dressing ingredients in a bowl. Next, stir in the salad ingredients and mix well. Serve.

Eggplant Salad

Preparation time: 10 minutes

Cook time: 10 minutes

Nutrition facts (per serving): 72 cal (5g fat, 1.4g protein, 2g fiber)

The eggplant salad makes a great side serving for the table, and you can serve as a delicious and healthy snack as well.

Ingredients (4 servings)

2 eggplants, sliced

2 tablespoon maple syrup

2 tablespoon soy sauce

Black pepper, to taste

¼ cup parsley, chopped

1 hot chili pepper, sliced

Preparation

Sauté the eggplant with oil in a skillet until golden brown. Add maple syrup, soy sauce, black pepper, parsley, and chili pepper. Mix well and serve.

Zucchini Dill Salad

Preparation time: 10 minutes
Nutrition facts (per serving): 56 cal (3.5g fat, 5.7g protein, 2g fiber)

The zucchini dill salad is another most popular salad in Israeli cuisine, and it has this great taste from the mix of zucchinis and spices.

Ingredients (4 servings)
4 zucchinis, coarsely grated
2 tablespoon olive oil
2 tablespoon white vinegar
2 tablespoon lemon juice
1 teaspoon sugar
2 garlic cloves, minced
¼ cup dill, chopped
Salt and black pepper to taste

Preparation
Toss the zucchini with olive oil, white vinegar, lemon juice, sugar, garlic cloves, dill, salt, and black pepper in a bowl. Serve.

Middle Eastern Carrot Salad

Preparation time: 10 minutes
Cook time: 10 minutes
Nutrition facts (per serving): 211 cal (20g fat, 4g protein, 13g fiber)

The carrot salad is the right fit to serve with all your Israeli entrees. Here the boiled carrots and radishes are mixed with garlic and red pepper, which makes a great combination.

Ingredients (4 servings)

4 carrots, shredded
½ cup black olives
7 radishes, shredded
1 red pepper, julienned
2 teaspoons garlic, minced
¼ teaspoon paprika
1 pinch cayenne pepper
1 pinch cinnamon
1 teaspoon salt
¼ cup fresh parsley, chopped
Juice of 1 lemon
⅓ cup olive oil

Preparation

Boil the carrots in a pot filled with salted water until soft. Drain and transfer the carrots to a salad bowl. Stir in the radishes, red peppers, and olives. Next, mix well. Add olive oil, lemon juice, parsley, salt, cinnamon, black pepper, and garlic in a small bowl. Pour this prepared mixture over the veggies and mix well. Cover and refrigerate for 30 minutes. Serve.

Jerusalem Artichoke Salad

Preparation time: 10 minutes
Cook time: 20 minutes
Nutrition facts (per serving): 253 cal (2g fat, 21g protein, 4g fiber)

Here comes a delicious and healthy salad, which has a refreshing twist due to the use of Jerusalem artichokes in it. It's delicious with beef skewers and kebabs.

Ingredients (6 servings)

¾ cup Jerusalem artichokes, sliced

½ onion, diced

½ cucumber, de-seeded and diced

1 garlic clove

1 tablespoon white vinegar

1 teaspoon Dijon mustard

3 tablespoon olive oil

1 cup arugula

2 cup cooked couscous, cooked

½ cup parsley, minced

Salt and black pepper to taste

Preparation

At 400 degrees F, preheat your oven. Toss the artichokes with black pepper, salt, and olive oil on a baking sheet. Next, roast for 20 minutes. Mix 1 tablespoon vinegar, 1 teaspoon Dijon mustard, and garlic in a salad bowl. Stir in 3 tablespoons olive oil, black pepper, and salt. Then mix well. Toss in the couscous, artichokes, parsley, arugula, cucumbers, and onions. Finally, mix well. Serve.

Israeli Cabbage Salad

Preparation time: 10 minutes
Nutrition facts (per serving): 176 cal (17g fat, 7g protein, 3g fiber)

As if the Israeli menu is incomplete without a cabbage salad. It's made out of cabbage and mayonnaise dressing, which add lots of nutritional value to this salad.

Ingredients (4 servings)
1 bag red cabbage, shredded
4 tablespoon light mayonnaise
1 tablespoon fresh lemon juice
¼ teaspoon salt
¼ teaspoon black pepper

Preparation
Toss all the Israeli cabbage salad ingredients in a salad bowl. Serve.

Figs Salad

Preparation time: 10 minutes
Nutrition facts (per serving): 155 cal (8g fat, 13g protein, 2g fiber)

If you haven't tried this figs salad before, then here comes a simple and easy to cook recipe that you can serve at home effortlessly.

Ingredients (6 servings)
Juice of 1 lemon
2 teaspoons white vinegar
½ teaspoon salt
⅛ teaspoon black pepper
¼ cup olive oil
3 Persian cucumbers, diced
1 ½ cups cherry tomatoes, quartered
7 ounces figs
5-ounce block feta cheese, diced
1 scallion, sliced
2 sprigs mint leaves, chopped
1 sprig oregano leaves, chopped
20 sprigs parsley leave, chopped

Preparation
Toss all the salad ingredients in a salad bowl. Serve.

Soups

Chickpea Chili Soup

Preparation time: 15 minutes
Cook time: 20 minutes
Nutrition facts (per serving): 338 cal (20g fat, 13g protein, 3g fiber)

Now you can quickly make a flavorsome chickpeas chili soup with red split lentils and serve as a fancy meal for yourself and your guest.

Ingredients (6 servings)

2 teaspoons cumin seeds

Large pinch of chili flakes

1 tablespoon olive oil

1 red onion, chopped

5 ounces red split lentils

3 ½ cups vegetable stock

14 ounces can tomato, whole or chopped

7 ounces can chickpeas, drained and rinsed

Garnish

1 small bunch coriander, chopped

4 tablespoons Greek yogurt

Preparation

Toast the cumin seeds and chili flakes in a dry skillet until golden. Stir in the olive oil and onion. Sauté for 5 minutes. Add the red split lentils and rest of the ingredients. Cook for 15 minutes on a simmer. Puree the soup with a blender. Garnish with coriander and yogurt. Serve warm.

Barley Lentil Vegetable Soup

Preparation time: 5 minutes
Cook time: 1 hour 50 minutes
Nutrition facts (per serving): 470 cal (28g fat, 36g protein, 1.7g fiber)

Try this barley lentil soup at dinner. This warming bowl of soup is best to serve during winters at festive dinners and lunches.

Ingredients (4 servings)
¾ cup barley
⅓ cup brown lentils
2 tablespoon olive oil
2 carrots, sliced
2 stalks celery, chopped
2 large onions, chopped
Salt and black pepper, to taste
1 (28 ounces) can diced tomatoes, chopped
½ bunch kale
1 can red kidney beans

Preparation
Add 2 ½ cups water, lentils, and barley to a saucepan and cook for 30 minutes on a simmer. Sauté the onion with carrots, ½ teaspoons salt, oil, ¼ teaspoons black pepper in a deep skillet for 20 minutes. Add the tomatoes, and cook for 60 minutes. Stir in the barley and lentils and then mix well. Add the kale and beans. Mix and serve warm.

Kubeh soup

Preparation time: 10 minutes
Cook time: 40 minutes
Nutrition facts (per serving): 373 cal (10g fat, 32g protein, 7g fiber)

The kubbeh soup is famous all over the Middle East, and it's also enjoyed in Israel because of its earthy mix of zucchini, carrots, and meatballs.

Ingredients (6 servings)

⅓ cup vegetable oil
1 onion, chopped
3 tablespoons tomato paste
3 carrots, cut into rounds
3 zucchinis, cut into rounds
2 tablespoons chicken soup powder
1 teaspoon paprika
1 tablespoon sugar
1 teaspoon lemon salt
1 teaspoon salt
½ teaspoon black pepper
10 cups water
1 package frozen kubbeh

Preparation

Add oil to a skillet and place it over medium heat. Stir in the onion and cook until it turns soft. Pour in the tomato paste and cook until heated. Add 10 cups of water to a soup pot. Stir in tomato-onion mixture and carrots. Let this mixture boil; then add the spices, kubbeh, and zucchini. Turn off the heat and keep the mixture covered for 30 minutes. Enjoy.

Main Dishes

Lamb and Swiss Chard Shakshuka

Preparation time: 15 minutes
Cook time: 36 minutes
Nutrition facts (per serving): 213 cal (20g fat, 9g protein, 7g fiber)

The Israeli lamb shakshuka is famous for its delicious combination of Swiss chard with lamb meatballs and a tomato mixture.

Ingredients (9 servings)

1-pound ground lamb
1 teaspoon paprika
1 teaspoon turmeric
1 teaspoon cumin
1 teaspoon cinnamon
3 scallions, chopped
3 tablespoons mint, chopped
1 tablespoon cilantro, chopped
2 tablespoons parsley, chopped
9 eggs
Salt, to taste
1 bunch Swiss chard, stem removed
1 tablespoon olive oil
1 onion, diced
6 garlic cloves, chopped
1 red pepper, cut into strips
1-pound matbucha
14-ounce canned diced tomatoes
1 Handful parsley, chopped
Freshly black pepper, to taste

Preparation

At 350 degrees F, preheat your oven. Mix the lamb with salt, 1 egg, parsley, cilantro, mint, scallions, cinnamon, cumin, turmeric, and paprika in a mixing bowl. Make 15 meatballs from this mixture and place them on a baking sheet with parchment paper. Next, bake for 20 minutes. Mix about 8 cups of water with 2 tablespoons salt in a pan and boil it. Add Swiss chard to the water and cook for 1 ½ minute. Drain the greens, squeeze, and chop them.

Sauté the onions with 1 tablespoon olive oil in a pan until soft. Stir in the garlic and sauté for 1 minute. Add the sliced pepper and cook for 3 minutes. Add the diced tomatoes and matbucha and cook for 5 minutes. Roll the Swiss chard into small balls. Add the Swiss chard balls to the pan. Make small wells in this mixture and place the lamb meatballs. Crack the eggs on top of meatballs, cover with a lid, and cook for 5 minutes. Drizzle black pepper and salt on top. Garnish with parsley. Serve warm.

Cauliflower with Tahini and Silan

Preparation time: 15 minutes
Cook time: 20 minutes
Nutrition facts (per serving): 181 cal (5g fat, 7g protein, 6g fiber)

If you haven't tried the cauliflower with tahini and silan before, then here comes a simple and easy to cook recipe to celebrate this cuisine!

Ingredients (4 servings)
1 cauliflower, cut into florets
¼ cup olive oil
Sea salt
3 tablespoons tahini
Lemon juice
3 teaspoons Silan (or other date syrup)
Chopped parsley
Pomegranate seeds or dried cranberries
Toasted pine nuts

Preparation
At 400 degrees F, preheat your oven. Spread the cut cauliflower on a baking sheet and bake for 20 minutes until golden brown. Toss the cauliflower with Silan, tahini, and lemon juice in a bowl. Garnish with pine nuts, pomegranate seeds, and parsley. Serve.

Zaatar Crusted Gefilte Fish

Preparation time: 15 minutes
Cook time: 45 minutes
Nutrition facts (per serving): 312 cal (16g fat, 13g protein, 1g fiber)

The Israeli zaatar-crusted gefilte fish is a delight to serve at the dinner table. It's beloved for its unique Zaatar, mixed with wasabi flavors.

Ingredients (4 servings)

1 loaf frozen gefilte fish
¾ cup Zaatar
½ teaspoon salt
1 pinch of black pepper
⅓ cup olive oil
1 teaspoon wasabi powder
Water
¼ cup mayonnaise

Preparation

At 350 degrees F, preheat your oven. Mix Zaatar with black pepper, salt, and olive oil in a bowl. Rub this mixture over the fish liberally and place it in a greased baking pan. Bake the Zaatar fish for 35 minutes, increase the temperature to 425 degrees F, and then bake for 10 minutes. Mix the wasabi powder with mayonnaise and water in a bowl. Serve the fish with aioli.

Steamed Cod with Olive Tapenade

Preparation time: 10 minutes
Cook time: 20 minutes
Nutrition facts (per serving): 350 cal (17g fat, 31g protein, 1g fiber)

Try this Israeli steamed cod with olive tapenade with your favorite herbs on top. Adding a dollop of cream or yogurt will make it even richer in taste.

Ingredients (4 servings)
2 (6 oz.) cod portions
¼ cup black olives, pitted
⅓ cup sundried tomatoes
2 garlic cloves, peeled and sliced
2 tablespoons olive oil
¼ cup white wine
Salt and black pepper, to taste

Preparation
At 375 degrees F, preheat your oven. Sauté the garlic with oil in a skillet for 5 minutes. Blend the tomatoes with an olive in a food processor. Add the sautéed garlic with its oil and blend well. Rub the fish with black pepper, salt and place it over the foil squares. Divide the olives mixture over the fish and wrap foil around. Place the packaged fish on a baking sheet and then bake for 20 minutes. Serve.

Capers Sea Bass

Preparation time: 10 minutes
Cook time: 12 minutes
Nutrition facts (per serving): 127 cal (4g fat, 6g protein, 2g fiber)

Enjoy this entree with a fresh vegetable salad. You can adjust spices according to your preference and make a perfect showcase for your dinner.

Ingredients (6 servings)

3 tablespoons capers, drained

8 sun-dried tomato slices

4 scallions, white parts, chopped

2 garlic cloves, peeled

Salt and black pepper, to taste

6 (6 ounces) sea bass fillets, skin removed

Preparation

Mix the garlic, scallions, salt, black pepper, capers, tomatoes, and their oils in a blender for 1 minute. Place the seabass fillets in the baking dish and spread the mixture over the fish. Cover it with aluminum foil and bake for 12 minutes at 400 degrees F. Serve warm.

Baked Trout with Fennel Salad

Preparation time: 10 minutes
Cook time: 18 minutes
Nutrition facts (per serving): 110 cal (11g fat, 2g protein, 6g fiber)

Make this baked trout in no time, and enjoy it with some garnish on top. Adding capers salad makes it super tasty.

Ingredients (4 servings)
Salad
2 fennel bulbs, sliced
2 tablespoon capers
1 lemon, juiced
¼ cup parsley leaves
2 tablespoon olive oil

Fish
6 whole small trouts, butterflied
1 small red onion, sliced
1 large lemon, sliced
1 small bunch of parsley
12 sprig fresh oregano
¼ cup olive oil
1 teaspoon salt
Black pepper, to taste

Preparation

Mix the capers, olive oil, parsley, lemon juice, and fennels in a small bowl. At 400 degrees F, preheat your oven. Place the trout on a greased baking tray and stuff the fish with red onion slices, oregano, parsley, and lemon. Rub the stuffed fish with salt, black pepper, and olive oil. Bake it for 18 minutes in the oven until flakey and serve with a capers salad.

Pan-Seared Salmon with Zaatar

Preparation time: 15 minutes
Cook time: 13 minutes
Nutrition facts (per serving): 336 cal (2g fat, 33 protein, 12g fiber)

This seared salmon with zaatar is quite famous in the region; in fact, and it's a must to try because of its nutritional content.

Ingredients (2 servings)

1 ½ pound of salmon, skinless, and cut into portions
1 teaspoon coarse salt
½ teaspoon black pepper
1 tablespoon oil
¼ cup soy sour cream
1 tablespoon Zaatar

Preparation

Preheat oil in a skillet for 3 minutes. Rub the salmon with black pepper and salt and sear the fish for 5 minutes per side. Serve the fish with sour cream and Zaatar on top. Enjoy.

Sabich Crostini

Preparation time: 15 minutes
Cook time: 22 minutes
Nutrition facts (per serving): 482 cal (4g fat, 28g protein, 3g fiber)

If you haven't tried the sabic crostini before, then here comes a simple and easy to cook this recipe that you can prepare at home easily.

Ingredients (4 servings)

Crostini
1 baguette
2 tablespoons olive oil
Salt
Black pepper
2 cloves garlic

Tahini Sauce
¼ cup tahini paste
1 tablespoon fresh lemon juice
Salt and pepper to taste

Eggplant
2 medium eggplants
2 tablespoons olive oil
2 tablespoons Zaatar
½ teaspoon salt

Israeli salad

½ cucumber, diced

2 plum tomatoes, diced

1 tablespoon red onion, diced

1 tablespoon cilantro, minced

2 teaspoons lemon juice

Salt, to taste

Black pepper, to taste

Preparation

At 400 degrees F, preheat your oven. Layer a baking sheet with foil. Slice the baguette into ¼ inch slices and brush them with olive oil, black pepper, and salt. Place these slices on the baking sheet, roast them for 7 minutes, and then flip them when cooked halfway through. Slice the eggplants and toss them with salt, Zaatar, and olive oil in a baking pan. Roast the eggplant for 15 minutes. Mix all the tahini sauce ingredients in a bowl and spread over the crostini. Add the roasted eggplant on top. Mix the Israeli salad ingredients in a bowl and divide over the crostini. Serve.

Cauliflower Couscous

Preparation time: 15 minutes
Nutrition facts (per serving): 358 cal (14g fat, 9g protein, 4g fiber)

You can give this cauliflower couscous a try because it has a good and delicious combination of grated cauliflower with tomatoes and olives.

Ingredients (4 servings)
½ large head of cauliflower
½ bunch parsley
¼ cup fresh mint
2 Roma tomatoes, seeded and diced
¼ cup black olives, chopped
¼ cup red onions, chopped
¼ cup lemon juice
3 tablespoons olive oil
1 garlic clove, minced
½ teaspoon of sea salt
¼ teaspoon cumin
¼ teaspoon smoked paprika
1 dash cayenne pepper

Preparation
Rice or grate the cauliflower in the food processor. Next, add parsley and the remaining ingredients. Mix well and serve.

Turmeric Rice

Preparation time: 15 minutes

Cook time: 17 minutes

Nutrition facts (per serving): 441 cal (11g fat, 34g protein, 5g fiber)

This turmeric rice is loved by all, young and adult. It's super simple and quick to make and served with all stews, soups, and curries.

Ingredients (4 servings)

4 ½ cups vegetable stock

2 cups basmati rice

¼ cup olive oil

1 tablespoon ground turmeric

2 teaspoons ground ginger

1 teaspoon salt

Fried mint leaves

1 bunch mint leaves

1 tablespoon coconut oil

Preparation

Add rice, vegetable stock, olive oil, turmeric, and the rest of the ingredients in a saucepan. Cook for 15 minutes on a simmer until the rice is soft. Fry mint leaves with coconut oil in a skillet for 2 minutes. Garnish the rice with the fried mint. Serve.

Lentil, Sausage, and Cabbage Cholent

Preparation time: 5 minutes
Cook time: 10 hours
Nutrition facts (per serving): 361 cal (20g fat, 11g protein, 0.8g fiber)

Have you ever tried cholent before? Well, here comes a loaded bowl of cabbage and lentil cholent, which is slow-cooked to get the best taste.

Ingredients (6 servings)

4 cups of water
1 can (28 ounces) crushed tomatoes, diced
4 sausage links, sliced
½ pound brown lentils, rinsed
1 onion, chopped
2 celery ribs, chopped
3 carrots, chopped
4 garlic cloves, minced
½ head green cabbage, shredded
1 bay leaf
1 teaspoon salt
¼ teaspoon black pepper
½ teaspoon white vinegar

Preparation

Add water, tomatoes, sausages, and all other ingredients to a slow cooker. Cover and cook the mixture for 10 hours on a Low setting. Serve warm.

Vegetable Cholent

Preparation time: 15 minutes
Cook time: 8 hours
Nutrition facts (per serving): 325 cal (20g fat, 6g protein, 2g fiber)

Do you want to enjoy an Israeli cholent in vegan style? Then try this Israeli vegetable cholent recipe. You can serve the cholent with toasted bread or rice.

Ingredients (6 servings)

2 cups assorted beans and lentils, soaked and drained
1 cup barley
1 celery root, peeled and cubed
1 parsnip, peeled and cubed
1 carrot, peeled and cubed
1 potato, cubed
1 sweet potato, peeled and diced
1 onion, chopped
5 garlic cloves, peeled
1 ½ teaspoon salt
1 teaspoon turmeric
1 teaspoon smoked Spanish paprika
½ teaspoon black pepper
1-pound beef stew meat, diced
1 bay leaf

Preparation

Add the beans, lentils, and barley to a slow cooker. Stir in water and other ingredients to the cooker. Cover and cook the cholent for 8 hours on Low heat setting. Discard the bay leaf and serve warm.

Date-Glazed Chicken Roast

Preparation time: 15 minutes
Cook time: 55 minutes
Nutrition facts (per serving): 624 cal (29g fat, 72g protein, 2g fiber)

The classic Israeli date glazed chicken roast is here to complete your Israeli menu. This meal can be served on all special occasions and festive celebrations.

Ingredients (6 servings)
8 ounces dried dates
1 cup orange juice
3 garlic cloves, chopped
2 tablespoon fresh thyme
2 tablespoon olive oil
1 tablespoon red wine vinegar
½ teaspoon ground cinnamon
½ teaspoon ground cumin
3-pound chicken, cut into pieces

Preparation
Soak all the dried dates in a bowl filled with warm water for 20 minutes; then peel them and remove their pits. Transfer the date's flesh to a blender. Add the cumin, cinnamon, vinegar, olive oil, thyme, garlic, and orange juice and then blend until smooth. Mix the chicken with the date mixture and spread it on a baking sheet. Bake for 25 minutes. Flip the chicken and bake for 25 minutes. Mist the pieces with cooking spray and broil for 5 minutes. Serve warm.

Falafel Crusted Chicken

Preparation time: 10 minutes
Cook time: 35 minutes
Nutrition facts (per serving): 471 cal (13g fat, 19g protein, 3g fiber)

Let's have a rich and delicious falafel crusted chicken. Try it with warm bread slices and tomato sauce, and you'll simply love it.

Ingredients (5 servings)
10 chicken drumsticks
1 cup dried falafel mix
2 tablespoon olive oil
Salt and black pepper, to taste

Tahini Sauce
½ cup tahini paste
¼ cup lemon juice
1 garlic clove, minced
½ teaspoon salt
¼ cup cold water

Preparation
At 475 degrees F, preheat your oven. Layer a baking sheet with a foil sheet and grease it with olive oil. Rub the chicken with black pepper, salt, and olive oil. Coat the chicken with the falafel mix and place the chicken in the baking tray. Bake the chicken for 15 minutes and then flip and bake for 20 minutes. Mix the tahini with lemon juice, garlic, water, and salt in a blender. Serve the chicken with the tahini sauce.

Pomegranate Chicken

Preparation time: 15 minutes
Cook time: 10 minutes
Nutrition facts (per serving): 349 cal (3.6g fat, 22g protein, 5.4g fiber)

It's about time to try some classic pomegranate chicken on the menu and make it more diverse and flavorsome. Serve warm with your favorite herbs on top.

Ingredients (4 servings)

2 tablespoons honey
3 limes, juiced
¾ cup pomegranate juice
1 cup canola oil
2 tablespoons sesame oil
4 (8 oz.) boneless and skinless chicken breasts
1 (12 oz.) package field greens
1 head radicchio, diced
2 cups arugula, chopped
1 cup sun-dried cranberries
½ toasted pecans
4 clementine oranges, cut in half
1 pomegranate, quartered and seeds kept
Salt, to taste
Black pepper, to taste

Preparation

Mix pomegranate juices with lime and honey in a small bowl. Stir in sesame oil, canola oil, black pepper, and salt, and then mix well. Pour ½ of the liquid into a sealable bag and place the chicken in the bag. Seal it and shake it well and refrigerate for 4 hours. Remove the marinated chicken from the Ziploc bag and discards its liquid. Set a grill over high heat and grease its grilling grates. Slice the chicken into 2 inches strips and grill them for 3-5 minutes per side. Prepare the salad and mix greens with arugula, radicchio, and the rest of the ingredients in a bowl. Serve the salad with the grilled chicken on top and garnish with the pomegranate seeds.

Israeli Classic Kebab

Preparation time: 10 minutes
Cook time: 20 minutes
Nutrition facts (per serving): 472 cal (29g fat, 31g protein, 1.4g fiber)

The famous kebab is here to make your meal special. You can always serve these kebabs with fresh cucumber or tomato salad.

Ingredients (4 servings)
1-pound ground lamb
1 onion, minced
1 chili pepper, minced
2 garlic cloves, minced
¼ cup parsley, chopped
1 teaspoon paprika
1 teaspoon sumac
½ teaspoon salt
¼ teaspoon black pepper
1 lemon, juiced

Preparation
Mix lamb with onion, chili pepper, garlic, parsley, paprika, sumac, salt, and black pepper in a bowl. Make long kebabs around wooden skewers. Place the prepared lamb skewers on a baking sheet and roast for 10 minutes in the Broiler on high heat. Flip the skewers and bake for 10 minutes. Garnish with lemon juice. Serve warm.

Lamb Meatballs with Tahini Sauce

Preparation time: 15 minutes

Cook time: 31 minutes

Nutrition facts (per serving): 420 cal (13g fat, 44g protein, 2g fiber)

These lamb meatballs taste amazing due to their combo with tahini sauce. Serve these meatballs with crispy nachos.

Ingredients (6 servings)

Tahini sauce

⅔ cup tahini paste

⅔ cup of water

4 ½ tablespoons white wine vinegar

1 garlic clove, minced

Pinch salt

Meatballs

2 pieces of white bread

10 ½ ounces ground beef

10 ½ ounces ground lamb

3 garlic cloves, minced

⅔ cup parsley, chopped

1 teaspoon salt

½ teaspoon black pepper

2 ½ teaspoons ground allspice

1 ½ teaspoons cinnamon

1 egg

Olive oil for frying

Zest of ½ lemon

Preparation

Mix all the ingredients for tahini sauce in a bowl and keep it aside. At 400 degrees F, preheat your oven. Soak bread in a bowl filled with cold water, remove it from the water and squeeze it. Transfer the bread to a large bowl. Stir in egg, spices, salt, parsley, garlic, and meat, and then mix well. Make small meatballs out of this mixture. Preheat 4 tablespoon olive oil in a deep skillet over medium-high heat. Sear the meatballs for 3 minutes per side. Bake the meatballs for 15 minutes, and then pour the tahini sauce on top. Bake for another 10 minutes. Garnish with lemon zest. Serve warm.

Chicken Shawarma

Preparation time: 15 minutes
Cook time: 16 minutes
Nutrition facts (per serving): 258 cal (6.4g fat, 29g protein, 1g fiber)

Chicken shawarma is always an easy way to add extra spice and nutrients to your menu, and here some that you can make in just a few minutes.

Ingredients (2 servings)

1-pound skinless, boneless chicken legs
⅓ cup canola oil
1 tablespoon turmeric
1 tablespoon ground coriander
1 teaspoon garlic powder
1 teaspoon cumin
1 teaspoon paprika
¼ teaspoon cinnamon
¼ teaspoon ground cloves
1 teaspoon salt
½ teaspoon black pepper
Flatbread to serve

Preparation

Cut the chicken into a strip and toss them with oil and spices in a bowl. Sauté the chicken in a pan for 8 minutes per side and transfer onto the flatbread in the serving plate. Serve warm.

Kataifi Nests with Ground Lamb

Preparation time: 15 minutes
Cook time: 49 minutes
Nutrition facts (per serving): 379 cal (13g fat, 25g protein, 3g fiber)

Here is a delicious and savory combination of lamb, and baked kataifi noodles that you must add to your menu.

Ingredients (4 servings)

6 ounces Kataifi
4 tablespoons olive oil
Oil spray
1 small onion, diced
3 garlic cloves, minced
1 small green zucchini, small dice
½-pound ground lamb meat
1 tablespoon mint, chopped
1 tablespoon parsley, chopped
1 tablespoon cilantro, chopped
1 tablespoon Jerusalem mix spice blend

Preparations

At 350 degrees F, preheat your oven. Rip and pull the kataifi into 2 inches long strips and place in a bowl. Grease the kataifi by mixing with 2 tablespoons of oil. Grease a suitable muffin pan with cooking spray and divide the kataifi into the muffin cups. Make a well at the center of each cup to make a nest. Bake the kataifi nest for 30 minutes until golden brown. Sauté the onions with 2 tablespoons olive oil in a pan. Stir in garlic and sauté for 45 seconds. Add prepared zucchini and cook for 5 minutes, then cook for 5 minutes. Stir in lamb and cook for 5 minutes. Add Jerusalem spice mix, whisk well and cook for 2 minutes. Stir in herbs and sauté for 1 minute. Remove the lamb from the heat and divide the lamb mixture in the kataifi nests and serve warm with the pine nuts and tahini.

Roasted Chicken with Rice

Preparation time: 15 minutes
Cook time: 90 minutes
Nutrition facts (per serving): 244 cal (6g fat, 8g protein, 5g fiber)

If you haven't tried this roasted chicken with currant rice, then here comes a simple and easy to cook recipe that you can recreate at home in no time with minimum efforts.

Ingredients (8 servings)
Stuffing
1-pound ground chicken
1 tablespoon olive oil
¼ teaspoon allspice
¼ teaspoon coriander
¼ teaspoon cinnamon
2 garlic cloves, chopped
½ teaspoon salt
¼ teaspoon black pepper
1 ½ cup cooked rice
3 tablespoon pine nuts
2 tablespoon currants
1 tablespoon fresh mint, chopped
Fresh mint sprigs for garnish

Chicken
1 whole chicken, giblets removed
½ teaspoon salt

½ teaspoon black pepper

4 carrots, peeled and julienned

2 small onions, peeled and diced

2 turnips, peeled and diced

2 cups chicken broth

Preparation

Sauté pine nuts in a dry skillet for 4 minutes until golden brown, then transfer to a bowl. Sauté ground chicken with olive oil, allspice, garlic, black pepper, salt, cinnamon, and coriander in the skillet for 6 minutes. Then remove this chicken mixture from the heat and stir in rice, mint, currants, and pine nuts. Mix well and keep the stuff aside. Stuff the prepared stuffing under the whole chicken's skin and place the chicken in the roasting pan. Roast the chicken for 30 minutes at 350 degrees F. Add vegetables and chicken broth around the chicken and roast for 60 minutes. Allow the chicken to rest, then slice and garnish with mint. Serve warm.

Roasted Chicken with Grilled Eggplant

Preparation time: 15 minutes
Cook time: 34 minutes
Nutrition facts (per serving): 336 cal (13g fat, 28g protein, 1.7g fiber)

A perfect mix of roasted chicken with grilled eggplant cooked with green olives and tomato paste. Serve warm with your favorite side salad for the best taste.

Ingredients (8 servings)
8 boneless chicken thighs
3 (8 ounces) grilled eggplant
2 tablespoons tomato paste
1 tablespoon Silan
16 ounces pitted green olives
1 pinch cayenne
1 lemon, juiced
¼ cup mint, chopped
Salt and black pepper, to taste

Preparation
At 400 degrees F, preheat your oven. Grease a grill pan with 2 tablespoon oil and heat over medium-high heat. Rub the chicken with black pepper and salt, then sear for 2 minutes per side. Remove this chicken from the heat and transfer to a baking pan. Add cayenne pepper, lemon juice, green olives, Silan, tomato paste, black pepper, salt, and grilled eggplant. Bake for 30 minutes, then garnish with mint. Serve.

Crusted Lamb Shoulder

Preparation time: 15 minutes
Cook time: 50 minutes
Nutrition facts (per serving): 316 cal (7g fat, 24g protein, 12g fiber)

The crusted lamb shoulder is famous for its unique taste and aroma, and now you can bring those exotic flavors home by using this recipe.

Ingredients (6 servings)
1 tablespoon salt
2 tablespoon parsley, minced
1 tablespoon thyme leaves, minced
1 tablespoon rosemary leaves, minced
5 garlic cloves, minced
2 tablespoon grainy mustard
1 tablespoon grated lemon zest
3 tablespoon olive oil
1 (3 ½-pound) shoulder of lamb, rolled, tied
1 cup beef stock
½ cup red wine
1 tablespoon cornstarch

Preparation
Mix mustard with oil, lemon zest, garlic, rosemary, thyme, parsley, and salt in a food processor to make a paste. Rub this mixture over the lamb, cover, and refrigerate for 1 hour. At 325 degrees F, preheat your oven. Place the lamb rack in a roasting pan and roast for 1 ½ hour, and pour in half of the wine and stock. Bake for another 30 minutes. Transfer the roasted lamb to a plate and cover it

with a foil. Transfer the lamb juices to a saucepan. Stir in wine and stock, and then cook over medium heat. Mix cornstarch with 2 tablespoons water in a bowl. Pour this slurry into the juices and cook for 5 minutes until the sauce thickens. Sauté 2 cups couscous with 2 tablespoons oil in a large skillet for 5 minutes. Stir in 3 cups chicken broth and cook for 10 minutes. Stir in parsley, mint leaves, and the rest of the ingredients. Mix well and serve the lamb with the couscous. Enjoy.

Sumac Beef Skewers

Preparation time: 15 minutes

Cook time: 10 minutes

Nutrition facts (per serving): 386 cal (11g fat, 32g protein, 3g fiber)

These sumac beef skewers are a must-have for every fancy dinner, and with the help of this recipe, you can cook them in no time.

Ingredients (2 servings)

¼ cup olive oil

1 tablespoon lemon juice

Zest of 1 orange

1 garlic clove, smashed

½-pound skirt steak, cut into strips

2 ripe mangoes, peeled and cubed

3 tablespoons olive oil

1 tablespoon lemon juice

1 tablespoon rice vinegar

1 teaspoon harissa

¼ cup red pepper, diced

¼ parsley, chopped

2 tablespoons fresh cilantro, chopped

¼ cup scallions, sliced

2 tablespoons sumac

1 tablespoon ground coriander

1 teaspoon black pepper

½ teaspoon ground cumin

1 pinch salt

Salt and black pepper, to taste

Preparation

Mix lemon juice, black pepper, salt, garlic, orange zest, and olive oil in a bowl. Thread the beef on the skewers and place them on a baking sheet. Pour the marinade over the beef. Cover and marinate the beef for 4 hours in the refrigerator. Blend mangoes in a blender until smooth. Add scallions, cilantro, parsley, red pepper, harissa, rice vinegar, lemon juice, and olive oil and mix well. Prepare and preheat a grill over medium heat. Mix salt, cumin, black pepper, sumac, and coriander in a small bowl. Drizzle this mixture over the skewers and grill them for 5 minutes per side and serve with mango chutney.

Beef Moussaka With Matbucha

Preparation time: 15 minutes
Cook time: 88 minutes
Nutrition facts (per serving): 428 cal (17g fat, 11g protein, 8g fiber)

The beef moussaka always tastes great when you cook and serve it with matbucha, all together with spices and breadcrumbs.

Ingredients (4 servings)
3 eggplants
3 tablespoons salt
2 tablespoons olive oil
2 onions, small dice
8 garlic cloves, minced
1 ½ pounds ground beef
2 tablespoons tomato paste
1 ½ teaspoon cumin
1 ½ teaspoon paprika
1 ½ teaspoon garlic powder
2 eggs
3 (8 oz.) Moroccan matbucha
½ cup Le'Pesach breadcrumbs
Salt and black pepper, to taste

Preparation
At 400 degrees F, preheat your oven. Layer a cookie sheet with a parchment sheet. Slice the eggplants and pat them dry. Spread the slices in the baking sheet and brush them with olive oil. Bake the eggplants for 25 minutes until golden

brown. Sauté the onions with 2 tablespoons olive oil in a saucepan for 5 minutes. Stir in garlic and sauté for 1 minute. Stir in ground beef and mix well. Add tomatoes, paste, and spices, and then cook for 7 minutes. Add eggs and mix well. Spread 2-3 tablespoons matbucha in a baking pan, top it with half of the eggplant slices and cover with half of the beef, then with remaining matbucha. Repeat the layers using the remaining ingredients. Mix breadcrumbs with salt and ¼ cup olive oil in a bowl. Spread this mixture over the eggplant layers. Cover the layers with aluminum foil and bake for 35 minutes. Remove the foil and bake for 15 minutes. Slice and serve warm.

Lamb Shawarma With Pomegranate Salsa

Preparation time: 15 minutes
Cook time: 20 minutes
Nutrition facts (per serving): 556 cal (28g fat, 68g protein, 10g fiber)

Are you in a mood to have lamb shawarma on this menu? Well, you can serve this lamb shawarma with the pomegranate salsa on top.

Ingredients (10 servings)

½ cup soy sour cream

1 lemon, juiced

1 tablespoon distilled white vinegar

1 tablespoon olive oil

½ cup onions, chopped

2 garlic cloves, minced

1 tablespoon salt

1 teaspoon black pepper

1 teaspoon ground cumin

1⁄2 teaspoon ground nutmeg

1⁄2 teaspoon ground cloves

1 teaspoon cayenne

5 pounds boneless shoulder lamb, cut into 1⁄4-inch strip

Preparation

Mix garlic, onions, olive oil, vinegar, lemon juice, ¼ cup water, and sour cream in a large bowl. Stir in cayenne, cloves, nutmeg, black pepper, and salt. Mix well and add lamb strips. Mix well to coat. Cover it with a plastic wrap or sheet and marinate for 24 hours in the refrigerator. Meanwhile, prepare the salad by mixing all its ingredients in a bowl, then cover and refrigerate for 2 hours. Preheat a suitable large skillet over high heat and sear the lamb strips for 5 minutes per side. Serve warm with salad and enjoy.

Chicken Chorizo Jambalaya

Preparation time: 10 minutes

Cook time: 46 minutes

Nutrition facts (per serving): 425 cal (28g fat, 33g protein, 2g fiber)

Have you tried the chicken chorizo jambalaya before? Well, now you can enjoy this unique and flavorsome combination of rice with chicken and chorizo by cooking this recipe at home.

Ingredients (6 servings)

1 tablespoon olive oil

2 chicken breasts, chopped

1 onion, diced

1 red pepper, sliced

2 garlic cloves, crushed

2 ½ ounces chorizo, sliced

1 tablespoon Cajun seasoning

9 ounces long grain rice

14 ounces can plum tomato

1 ½ cups chicken stock

Preparation

Sauté 2 chopped chicken breasts with 1 tablespoon olive oil in a pan for 8 minutes, then transfer to a plate. Add onion to the same pan and sauté for 4 minutes. Stir in Cajun seasoning, chorizo, garlic, and red pepper. Sauté for 5 minutes. Stir in sautéed chicken, rice, tomatoes, and chicken stock. Cover and cook on a simmer for 25 minutes until rice is soft. Enjoy.

Root Lentil Casserole

Preparation time: 15 minutes
Cook time: 32 minutes
Nutrition facts (per serving): 443 cal (16g fat, 23g protein, 0.6g fiber)

This root lentil casserole is always served as a complete meal, and this one, in particular, is great to have on a nutritious diet.

Ingredients (8 servings)
2 tablespoons sunflower oil
1 onion, chopped
2 garlic cloves, crushed
24 ½ ounces potatoes, peeled and cut into chunks
4 carrot, sliced
2 parsnip, sliced
2 tablespoons curry paste
4 cups vegetable stock
3 ½ ounces red lentils
1 small bunch coriander, chopped
Yurt and naan bread, to serve

Preparation
Sauté garlic and onion with oil in a large pan for 4 minutes. Stir in parsnips, carrots, and potatoes and sauté for 7 minutes. Add stock and curry paste and reduce the heat. Add lentils, cover, and cook on a simmer for 20 minutes until lentils are soft. Add coriander and seasoning. Cook for 1 minute and garnish with yogurt and coriander. Serve warm.

Falafel Burgers

Preparation time: 10 minutes
Cook time: 10 minutes
Nutrition facts (per serving): 321 cal (20g fat, 24g protein, g fiber)

Falafel burgers are always great to serve on a vegan menu. Now you can make them easily at home by using the following simple ingredients.

Ingredients (4 servings)

14 ounces can chickpeas, rinsed drained
1 small red onion, chopped
1 garlic clove, chopped
A handful of parsley
1 teaspoon ground cumin
1 teaspoon ground coriander
½ teaspoons harissa paste
2 tablespoons plain flour
2 tablespoons sunflower oil
Toasted pitta bread, to serve
7 ounces tomato salsa, to serve
Green salad, to serve

Preparation

Drain and add the canned chickpeas to a food processor. Add salt, flour, harissa paste, coriander, cumin, parsley, garlic, and onion. Blend until smooth and make four patties out of this mixture. Place a suitable cooking pan over medium heat and add the sunflower oil. Sear the patties for 3 minutes per side until golden brown. Serve warm with pitta bread, green salad, and tomato salsa. Enjoy.

Rice and Lentils (Majadara)

Preparation time: 10 minutes
Cook time: 53 minutes
Nutrition facts (per serving): 207 cal (7.6g fat, 7g protein, 4g fiber)

If you haven't tried the rice and lentils majadara before, then here comes a simple and easy to cook a recipe that you can recreate at home in no time with minimum efforts.

Ingredients (6 servings)

¼ cup olive oil
1 onion, chopped
3 garlic cloves, chopped
1 teaspoon ginger root, chopped
1 cup of brown rice
1 cup green lentils
1 teaspoon ground cumin
1 teaspoon salt
½ teaspoon black pepper
½ teaspoon ground cinnamon
2½ cups water

Preparation

Sauté the garlic and onion with olive oil in a cooking pot for 7 minutes. Stir in ginger and sauté for 1 minute. Add brown rice and mix well. Add cinnamon, black pepper, salt, cumin, and lentils and pour water to cover the rice. Cover the lid and cook for 45 minutes on a low simmer. Serve warm.

Rice with Black Beans and Chickpeas

Preparation time: 10 minutes
Cook time: 26 minutes
Nutrition facts (per serving): 453 cal (12g fat, 31g protein, 3g fiber)

These black beans chickpeas rice are one delicious way to complete your Israeli menu; here is a recipe that you can try to have this delicious meal in no time.

Ingredients (8 servings)

1 tablespoon olive oil
1 garlic clove, minced
1 cup basmati rice
2 teaspoons ground cumin
2 teaspoons ground coriander
1 teaspoon ground turmeric
1 teaspoon ground cayenne pepper
1-quart chicken stock
1½ pound ground turkey
2 (15 ounce) cans garbanzo beans, drained
2 (15 ounces) cans black beans, drained
1 bunch cilantro, chopped
1 bunch fresh parsley, chopped
¼ cup pine nuts
Salt and black pepper to taste

Preparation

Sauté the garlic with olive oil in a saucepan for 1 minute. Stir in cayenne pepper, turmeric, coriander, cumin, and rice. Cook for 5 minutes and pour in chicken stock. Cook for 20 minutes on a simmer. Sauté the turkey in a greased skillet until golden brown. Transfer the turkey to the rice, then add black beans, garbanzo beans, parsley, cilantro, salt, black pepper, and pine nuts, then mix well. Serve warm.

Shabbat Fish

Preparation time: 15 minutes
Cook time: 1 hour
Nutrition facts (per serving): 278 cal (12g fat, 36g protein, 2g fiber)

The saucy Shabbat fish is a must to have the Israeli cuisine. Sure, it takes some time to get it ready, but it's a great taste worth all the time and effort.

Ingredients (6 servings)

1 red bell pepper, julienned
3 tomatoes, sliced
6 (6 ounces) tilapia fillets
2 tablespoons paprika
1 tablespoon chicken bouillon granules
1 teaspoon cayenne pepper
Salt and pepper to taste
¼ cup olive oil
1 cup water
¼ cup fresh parsley, chopped

Preparation

At 200 degrees F, preheat your oven. Spread the bell pepper and tomatoes in a baking dish and place the tilapia over the veggies. Mix olive oil, water, black pepper, salt, cayenne, chicken bouillon, and paprika in a bowl. Spread this mixture over the fish and drizzle parsley on top. Cover this baking dish with aluminum foil and bake for 1 hour until the fish is flaky. Serve.

Eggplant Chicken Pitas

Preparation time: 15 minutes
Cook time: 20 minutes
Nutrition facts (per serving): 492 cal (18g fat, 23g protein, 4g fiber)

When you can't think of anything to serve in the lunch or dinner, then these chicken pitas will help you big time.

Ingredients (6 servings)

2 eggplants, sliced
1 tablespoon salt
2 (6 ounces) boneless chicken breast halves
All-purpose flour for dusting
2 eggs, beaten
1 cup seasoned bread crumbs
4 tablespoons olive oil
3 garlic cloves, peeled
2 tablespoons red wine vinegar
2 tablespoons olive oil
1 (12 ounces) jar roasted red peppers, sliced
Salt and black pepper to taste
6 (6-inch) pita bread

Preparation

Place the cut eggplant slices in a colander and drizzle salt on top. Leave them for 20 minutes. Meanwhile, preheat and prepare a grill over medium-high heat. Place the chicken breasts in between two plastic sheets and pound them into ¼ inch thickness. Coat the chicken with the flour, dip them in the egg, and coat with breadcrumbs. Preheat about 2 tablespoons oil in a skillet over medium-high heat and sear the chicken for 5 minutes per side until golden brown. Transfer the chicken to a plate. Pat dry the eggplants and grill them for 5 minutes per side. Crush garlic with salt in a mortar with a pestle. Stir in olive oil, red wine vinegar and mix well. Transfer this mixture to a bowl. Add the eggplants and peppers and then mix well. Serve warm with chicken and pitas. Enjoy.

Curried Israeli Couscous

Preparation time: 10 minutes
Cook time: 15 minutes
Nutrition facts (per serving): 174 cal (4g fat, 5g protein, 1g fiber)

Try this super tasty Israeli couscous to serve with your meals, and you will never stop having it; that's how heavenly this couscous recipe tastes.

Ingredients (4 servings)

2 tablespoons olive oil

¼ cup minced onion

2 cubes vegetable bouillon

1 teaspoon yellow curry powder

½ teaspoon oregano

2 cups Israeli couscous

2½ cups water

Preparation

Sauté the onion with olive oil, oregano, curry powder, and bouillon cubes in a cooking pot for 5 minutes. Add couscous and water and cook the mixture to a boil, and then reduce the heat. Cover and cook for 10 minutes on a simmer. Serve warm.

Chopped Liver

Preparation time: 10 minutes
Cook time: 25 minutes
Nutrition facts (per serving): 241 cal (12g fat, 16g protein, 2g fiber)

The bowl of the chopped liver with boiled eggs and onions on top makes a great entrée. Serve it with toasted crispy bread and fresh cucumber salad.

Ingredients (4 servings)
Chopped liver
1 2/3 lbs. beef liver, diced
Salt and white pepper to taste
1½ medium onions, peeled and sliced
Vegetable oil for frying
2 hard-boiled eggs, shelled
2 tablespoons of vegetable oil
Egg and onion
½ medium onion, peeled and chopped
6 hard-boiled eggs, peeled and chopped
3 spring onions, sliced
4 tablespoons of vegetable oil
1 tablespoon of mayonnaise
¼ teaspoon of salt
¼ teaspoon of ground white pepper

Preparation
Toss diced eggs with spring onions and onion in a bowl. Add salt, pepper, vegetable oil, and mayonnaise, mix well and keep it aside. Sauté liver cubes in the

vegetable oil in a wok until they lose pink color. Transfer the liver to a plate and sauté onion until brown, and then keep them aside. Pass boiled eggs, onions, and liver through a mincer two times until finely minced. Mix the minced liver mixture with oil and adjust seasoning with salt and pepper. Serve with eggs and onion mixture. Enjoy.

Tahdig

Preparation time: 10 minutes
Cook time: 30 minutes
Nutrition facts (per serving): 261 cal (10g fat, 8g protein, 1g fiber)

The Tahdig is an essential part of all the Middle Eastern cuisine, including Israeli meals. Try this quick and easy recipe to serve in no time.

Ingredients (4 servings)

4 cups of water
1 cup basmati rice
½ cup Greek yogurt
1 teaspoon kosher salt
⅛ teaspoon crushed saffron threads
1 ½ tablespoons unsalted butter
2 teaspoons canola oil

Preparation

Add about 4 cups water to a stock pan and place it over medium-high heat. First, boil and then add the rice, and cook for 10 minutes. Rinse it under cold water. Whisk the yogurt with saffron and salt in a large bowl. Add the rice to the yogurt mixture and mix well. Melt the butter in a sauté pan, placed over medium heat. Stir in the oil and yogurt rice. Wrap a clean kitchen towel around the lid. Place this wrapped lid over the sauté pan and let the rice cook for 20 minutes on medium heat. Reduce the pan's heat to low and cook for another 20 minutes. Flip the pan over the serving plate and transfer the rice to this plate. Serve warm.

Saffron Fish

Preparation time: 10 minutes
Cook time: 30 minutes
Nutrition facts (per serving): 431 cal (24g fat, 15g protein, 6g fiber)

The saffron fish is served with tahini and nuts topping, which makes it a flavorsome and rich meal to serve at the dinner.

Ingredients (4 servings)

½ cup tahini
¼ cup lemon juice
¼ cup warm water
2 garlic cloves, grated
¼ cup pine nuts
1 tablespoon butter
Chopped parsley
Salt and black pepper, to taste

Preparation

Season the fish fillets with salt, black pepper, and oil. Next, place them in a baking dish. Bake this fish for 25 minutes at 375 degrees F in the oven. Mix the tahini, water, lemon juice, salt, pepper, and garlic in a suitable bowl. Melt the butter in a suitable pan over medium heat, and then add the pine nuts. Stir and cook for 5 minutes and then keep the nuts aside. Place the cooked fish on a serving plate and top it with tahini sauce, pine nuts, and parsley. Enjoy.

Fish Stew

Preparation time: 10 minutes
Cook time: 30 minutes
Nutrition facts (per serving): 358 cal (11g fat, 21g protein, 4g fiber)

This warming fish stew makes a complete meal for your dinner when served with crispy bread and mashed potatoes on the side.

Ingredients (4 servings)
6 fish fillets (about 4 oz. each), such as sea bass or grouper
3 tablespoon fresh lemon juice
1/4 cup olive oil
10 cloves garlic, roughly chopped
3 small red Thai chili, stemmed and roughly chopped
1 (6-oz) can tomato paste
2 cups minced cilantro
Salt and ground black pepper, to taste

Preparation
Season and rub the fish with salt, black pepper, and lemon juice in a suitable bowl. Preheat a 12-inch skillet with cooking oil over medium-high heat. Add chili and garlic, sauté for 2 minutes, and then add the tomato paste. Cook for 2 minutes, and then add cilantro and 1 ¼ cups water. Let it cook to a boil, and then reduce heat to a simmer. Cook for 6 minutes. Place the seasoned fish in the skillet with the skin side up. Cover this fish and cook for 20 minutes. Enjoy.

Lamb goulash

Preparation time: 10 minutes
Cook time: 2 hours 10 minutes
Nutrition facts (per serving): 364 cal (12g fat, 24g protein, 3g fiber)

The lamb goulash is another Middle Eastern recipe that's equally famous in Israeli. This one is cooked from a luscious mix of lamb and mushrooms.

Ingredients (6 servings)

2 ½ lbs. diced lamb leg

⅓ cup seasoned flour

2 tablespoon olive oil

1 large, sliced onion

2 cloves crushed garlic

1 tablespoon smoked paprika

1 lb. can condense tomato soup

½ cup red wine

1 teaspoon chili flakes

½ lb. button mushrooms, trimmed

1 red capsicum, deseeded, diced

¼ cup light sour cream

Parsley leaves to serve

Preparation

Let your oven preheat at 320 degrees F. Toss the lamb with flour to coat well and sear it in half of the oil in a large pan. Cook it for 4 minutes per side until brown, and then transfer it to a plate. Add the remaining oil to a pan and place it on high heat. Stir in the onion and sauté for 3 minutes. Add the paprika and cook for 1 minute. Pour in the soup, chili, and wine, let it, and boil then return the lamb to the pan. Cover it and bake for 1.5 hours in the oven. Toss in the capsicum and mushrooms and then cover again to bake for 30 minutes more. Add the sour cream and adjust the seasoning with salt. Garnish with parsley and cream. Enjoy.

Desserts

Tahini Pomegranate Thumbprint Cookies

Preparation time: 10 minutes
Cook time: 16 minutes
Nutrition facts (per serving): 167 cal (8g fat, 7g protein, 3g fiber)

These cookies are everything I was looking for. The mildly sweet cinnamon infused cookies taste great when baked with a pomegranate filling in the center.

Ingredients (12 servings)
Cookies
2/3 cup light brown sugar
2/3 cup butter
½ cup tahini paste
1 teaspoon vanilla bean paste
5 tablespoon heavy cream
2 large eggs
3 cups all-purpose flour
½ teaspoon salt
2 teaspoon ground cinnamon, roasted
1 teaspoon ground cardamom, roasted

Thumbprint Filling
½ cup pomegranate molasses
½ cup confectioners' sugar
½ teaspoon salt

Preparation

At 375 degrees F, preheat your oven. Next, beat the butter with sugar in a mixer until fluffy. Add the eggs and continue mixing for a minute. Stir in the cream, vanilla, and tahini, and then mix well. Add cardamom, cinnamon, salt, and flour and whisk until smooth. Cover and refrigerate this dough for 2 hours. Meanwhile, prepare the filling, and cook the pomegranate molasses in a saucepan over high heat until it bubbles. Stir in the sugar and cook for 1 minute with occasional stirring. Spread the parchment paper on two baking sheets and divide the prepared dough into 2 teaspoons balls. Place the balls into cookies and place them on the baking sheet. Make an indentation at the center of the cookies and divide the prepared filling into the cookies. Bake the cookies for 13 minutes, and then allow them to cool. Serve.

Israeli Charoset

Preparation time: 10 minutes
Nutrition facts (per serving): 185 cal (8g fat, 2.9g protein, 3g fiber)

The Israeli charoset is loved by all, the old and the young, and it makes a healthy dessert due to the mix of apples with bananas and dates.

Ingredients (10 servings)

2 apples, cored and quartered
3 bananas, peeled and diced
1 cup dates, pitted
1 cup walnuts, chopped
1 orange, zested and juiced
1 lemon, zested and juiced
2 teaspoons ground cinnamon
2 teaspoons white sugar
⅓ cup dry red wine
2 tablespoons matzo meal

Preparation

Blend the sugar, cinnamon, lemon juice and zest, orange zest, walnuts, dates, bananas, and apples in a food processor until chunky. Stir in the wine and mix well. Mix the apple mixture and matzo in a bowl. Cover and refrigerate for 30 minutes. Serve.

Tahini Olive Oil Cake

Preparation time: 10 minutes
Cook time: 35 minutes
Nutrition facts (per serving): 379 cal (11g fat, 34g protein, 3g fiber)

If you haven't tried the tahini olive oil cake before, then here comes a simple and easy to cook recipe that you can assemble on your own in no time with minimum efforts.

Ingredients (6 servings)
½ cup olive oil
½ cup honey
½ cup of sugar
½ cup Classic Tahini
2 tablespoons lemon juice
2 tablespoons lemon zest
1 ½ cups all-purpose flour
1 teaspoon ground cinnamon
1 teaspoon baking powder
½ teaspoon baking soda
½ teaspoon cardamom
¼ teaspoon nutmeg
¼ teaspoon salt

Preparation
At 350 degrees F, preheat your oven. Grease an 8-inch round cake pan with cooking spray and layer it with parchment paper. Blend the honey, olive oil, and sugar in a mixer until creamy. Stir in lemon zest, lemon juice and tahini. Mix

well, and then add the baking powder, salt, nutmeg, cardamom, baking soda, cinnamon, and flour, then mix until smooth. Spread this batter in the cake pan and bake for 35 minutes. Allow the cake to cool, slice, and serve.

Apple Honey Sorbet

Preparation time: 15 minutes

Cook time: 5 minutes

Nutrition facts (per serving): 188 cal (0.1g fat, 0.5g protein, 2g fiber)

If you want some new flavors on your dessert menu, then this apple honey sorbet recipe is best to bring variety to the menu.

Ingredients (4 servings)

1 ¼ pounds apples, cored and sliced

1 ½ cups water

1 ½ cups sugar

1 ½ lemon, juiced

1 tablespoon honey

Preparation

Mix the apples with lemon juice from ½ a lemon in a Ziploc bag and seal to refrigerate overnight. Boil the water with sugar in a suitable saucepan and cook for 5 minutes and then remove it from the heat. Stir in the honey, mix well, and allow the mixture to cool. Blend the apple in a blender until smooth. Add lemon juice and sugar syrup, and then blend well. Transfer this mixture to an ice-cream machine and freeze as per the directions. Serve.

Peanut Butter Bamba Mousse

Preparation time: 15 minutes
Cook time: 16 minutes
Nutrition facts (per serving): 347 cal (5g fat, 7g protein, 5g fiber)

A dessert that has no parallel, the Israeli peanut butter Bamba mousse is made with a peanut butter mousse and crunchy brittle to give you a delightful combination.

Ingredients (4 servings)
Roasted peanut brittle
5 ounces roasted peanuts, crushed
⅓ cup all-purpose flour
½ teaspoons black pepper
½ cup of brown sugar
½ cup of unsalted margarine

Peanut butter mousse
1 ½ cups peanut butter
3 cups whipping cream
½ cup confectioner sugar
1 teaspoon ginger
½ teaspoons salt
1 ½ tablespoons vanilla extract

Preparation
Mix the brown sugar, black pepper, flour, and crushed peanuts in a bowl. At 350 degrees F, preheat your oven. Mix the peanut blend with margarine in a

mixer and then spread this mixture on a baking sheet lined with parchment paper. Bake this crust for 15 minutes. Meanwhile, beat the peanut butter with cream in a bowl and heat for 30 seconds in the microwave. Stir in salt, ginger, and vanilla, and then beat on medium speed until smooth. Add the sugar and blend until incorporated. Divide half of the baked crust into ten small serving goblets. Top the crust with the creamy mousse. Garnish with the remaining crust. Serve.

Israeli Cheesecake

Preparation time: 15 minutes
Nutrition facts (per serving): 221 cal (3 g fat, 4 g protein, 2.8g fiber)

Yes, you can make something as delicious as this Israeli Cheesecake by using only basic dessert ingredients and some simple techniques.

Ingredients (12 servings)

13 ounces biscuit cookies, crushed

2 ½ ounces butter

2 teaspoons Nescafé powder

1 cup of sugar

26 ½ ounces Israeli white cheese

14 ounces sour cream

2 cups heavy cream

2 tablespoons instant vanilla pudding

Preparation

Add 2/3 crushed cookies, butter, 1 teaspoon Nescafe powder, and ⅓ cup sugar to a food processor, and then blend until evenly mixed. Spread this mixture in a 10-inch springform lined with parchment paper. Beat the heavy cream with instant pudding and remaining in a mixer until smooth. Spread this mixture in the prepared crust. Cover the cake with plastic wrap and refrigerate it overnight. Mix the remaining crushed cookies and Nescafe powder in a bowl. Spread this coffee cookie mixture on top of the cake. Slice and serve.

Limonana Bars

Preparation time: 15 minutes
Cook time: 75 minutes
Nutrition facts (per serving): 357 cal (12g fat, 5.5g protein, 1.4g fiber)

Try these limonana bars on this special dessert menu. The sweet combination of sugar, flour, eggs, and a basic flour crust tastes heavenly.

Ingredients (12 servings)
Crust
½ cup confectioners' sugar
1 ½ cups all-purpose flour
6 ounces margarine

Filling
2 ¼ cups sugar
2 cups fresh spearmint leaves
½ cup all-purpose flour
1 ⅛ cup lemon juice
Zest from 2 lemons
6 whole eggs
2 egg yolks
Confectioner's sugar for topping

Preparation
At 350 degrees F, preheat your oven. Grease a 9x13 inches baking pan with butter. Mix sugar with flour and margarine to prepare the crust. Spread this flour mixture into the prepared pan and cover the crust with parchment paper.

Bake it for 35 minutes in the oven. Meanwhile, prepare the filling. Blend sugar with mint in a food processor. Stir in the flour and mix well. Add the remaining ingredients and mix well. Remove the hot baked crust from the oven and remove the parchment paper from the top. Spread the prepared filling in the crust and bake for 40 minutes at 300 degrees F. Slice the cake into squares and garnish with sugar. Serve.

Israeli Jelly Donuts (Sufganiyot)

Preparation time: 10 minutes
Cook time: 15 minutes
Nutrition facts (per serving): 425 cal (17g fat, 5g protein, 0.8g fiber)

The Israeli jelly donuts will leave you spellbound due to their mildly sweet taste and a delicious jam filling inside.

Ingredients (10 servings)
2 cups all-purpose flour
¼ cup granulated sugar
1 (¼-ounce) packet active dry yeast
½ teaspoon salt
2 large egg yolks
¾ cup warm milk
2 tablespoons unsalted butter
6 cups vegetable oil, for frying
⅔ cup smooth jam
Powdered sugar, for dusting

Preparation
Mix the flour, yeast, salt, and sugar in a stand mixer's bowl. Stir in the milk and yolks, and then beat until it makes a shaggy dough. Add the butter and knead for 5 minutes. Transfer the prepared dough to a suitable greased bowl. Cover with a plastic sheet or wrap and leave it for 2 hours. Knead the prepared dough and spread it over a floured surface into ¼ inch thick. Cut the prepared dough sheet into doughnuts using a 2-inch round cookie cutter. Gather and roll the remaining dough and slice more doughnuts out of it. Place the prepared

doughnuts on a greased baking sheet and leave them for 30 minutes, covered with a kitchen towel. Preheat oil in a deep-frying pan to 350 degrees F. Deep fry the prepared doughnuts in the oil until golden brown. Transfer them to a colander using a spatula and let the excess oil drain. Don't hold the prepared doughnuts with your hands to avoid deflating them. Add the jam to piping and inject into each doughnut from one side. Dust them with sugar and enjoy.

Kachol Cheesecake Squares

Preparation time: 15 minutes
Cook time: 64 minutes
Nutrition facts (per serving): 169 cal (12g fat, 8g protein, 4g fiber)

The famous Israeli Kachol cheesecake squares are essential to try on the Israeli dessert menu. Try cooking them at home with these healthy ingredients and enjoy!

Ingredients (6 servings)

Crust

13 ounces chocolate wafers, crushed
¼ cup butter, melted
Butter to grease dish

Filling

2 eggs
1 cup of sugar
1 pound 5% gvina Levana
1 teaspoon vanilla extract
1 tablespoon potato starch

Topping

3 drops blue food coloring

Preparation

At 350 degrees F, preheat your oven. Crush the crumbs in a food processor. Add ¼ cup butter, and then mix well. Spread the mixture in an 8x8 inches baking dish and bake for 9 minutes. Prepare the filling by beating all these ingredients in a mixer until fluffy. Transfer ¼ batter to a bowl. Add food coloring to this batter and mix well. Spread the remaining batter onto the baked crust, dot the colored batter on top, and make swirls using a toothpick. Bake the cake for 55 minutes. Slice into squares and serve.

Tahini Butter Cookies

Preparation time: 5 minutes
Cook time: 15 minutes
Nutrition facts (per serving): 66 cal (5g fat, 0.8g protein, 2g fiber)

The Israeli tahini cookies will make your day with their delightful taste. Serve fresh with some hot beverages.

Ingredients (25 servings)

½ cup butter
¼ cup white sugar
½ teaspoon vanilla extract
¼ cup tahini
⅔ cup all-purpose flour
¼ teaspoon baking powder

Preparation

At 325 degrees F, preheat your oven. Beat sugar and butter in a mixer's bowl until fluffy. Stir in tahini and vanilla, and then mix well. Mix baking powder and flour in a bowl and stir in the butter mixture. Mix well and divide the mixture onto a greased cookie sheet into 1 tablespoon-sized cookies. Bake them for 15 minutes. Allow the cookie to cool and serve.

Semolina Cake (Basbousa)

Preparation time: 10 minutes
Cook time: 32 minutes
Nutrition facts (per serving): 408 cal (20g fat, 34g protein, 0.4g fiber)

If you want something exotic on your dinner table, then nothing can taste better than this delicious semolina cake.

Ingredients (6 servings)

3 eggs
4 teaspoons baking powder
4 teaspoons vanilla sugar
1 cup semolina
1 cup flour
Juice of 3 oranges
¾ cup oil
1 cup coconut flakes
1 cup of sugar
3 tablespoons honey
1 tablespoon lemon juice
1 cup boiling water
Silan (date syrup)
Nuts

Preparation

At 350 degrees F, preheat your oven. Beat the eggs with baking powder in a bowl. Stir in the sugar, coconut flakes, orange juice oil, semolina, and vanilla sugar. Mix well and spread the batter in a greased baking pan for 30 minutes.

Mix the water, lemon juice, and honey in a saucepan and cook for 2 minutes. Pour this mixture over the cake and garnish with nuts and Silan. Slice and serve.

Israeli Tiramisu

Preparation time: 10 minutes
Nutrition facts (per serving): 202 cal (7g fat, 6g protein, 1.3g fiber)

If you're a tiramisu fan, then this Israeli dessert recipe is the right fit for you. Try this at home and cook in no time.

Ingredients (8 servings)

3 cups heavy cream
¼ cup sugar
2 (3 ½ -ounce) envelopes instant vanilla pudding
1 ¾ cups whole milk
½ cup farmer's cheese
½ cup ricotta
¾ cup brewed espresso coffee, cooled
1 tablespoon cocoa powder
40 petit beurre cookies

Preparation

Beat sugar with cream in a mixer until it makes soft peaks. Mix 1 ½ cups milk with instant pudding in a large bowl. Stir in ricotta and farmer cheese. Mix well and stir in whipped cream. Mix ¼ cup milk with espresso and 1 tablespoon cocoa powder in a shallow bowl. Spread the cookies in a 9 inches baking pan in a single layer and pour ⅓ espresso mixture on top. Add ⅓ pudding mixture on top and repeat the layers. Drizzle cocoa powder on top. Cover with a plastic wrap or sheet and refrigerate overnight. Slice and serve.

Vegan Malabi

Preparation time: 10 minutes
Cook time: 8 minutes
Nutrition facts (per serving): 493 cal (18g g fat, 9g protein, 3g fiber)

The famous vegan Malabi is another special dessert to try on the Israeli menu. Try cooking it at home with these healthy ingredients and enjoy it.

Ingredients (4 servings)

3 tablespoons sugar

3 ½ tablespoons corn flour

1 cup almond milk

1 ½ teaspoons rose water

14 ounces of coconut milk

½ cup grenadine

1 pomegranate, seeds

Preparation

Mix 3 tablespoons of almond milk, corn flour, and sugar in a jug. Stir in rose water, and then keep the mixture aside. Mix the coconut milk and remaining almond milk in a saucepan and cook the mixture to boil. Remove this hot pan from the heat and stir in corn flour mixture, then mix well until smooth. Cook this mixture on a simmer for 1 minute until it thickens. Divide the mixture into serving glasses and cover with a plastic sheet. Refrigerate the Malabi and garnish with grenadine. Serve.

Baklava Bites

Preparation time: 15 minutes
Cook time: 55 minutes
Nutrition facts (per serving): 201 cal (6g fat, 4g protein, 0.6g fiber)

The baklava bites have no parallel; the crispy phyllo sheets make an interesting combination with the crunchy pistachio filling and sugary syrup.

Ingredients (6 servings)
Filling
1 pack phyllo dough
2 pounds of walnuts
1 tablespoon cinnamon
½ cup of sugar
¾ cup melted coconut oil
4 tablespoons pistachios, chopped

Syrup
1 cup of sugar
1 ½ cup of water
1 tablespoon rose water

Preparation
At 325 degrees F, preheat your oven. Mix sugar and water in a suitable saucepan and boil. Cook for 10 minutes, remove it from the heat, and add rose water. Mix well and allow the mixture to cool. Blend the walnuts in a food processor with cinnamon and sugar until coarsely ground. Spread a phyllo sheet on the working surface and brush it with coconut oil. Repeat the phyllo and coconut oil layers.

Cut these layers in half. Add half of the walnut mixture at the center of each pile of phyllo sheets and roll them into a log to seal the walnut filling inside. Slice the log into slices and place them on a baking sheet. Bake for 45 minutes in the oven until golden. Pour the prepared sugar syrup on top. Garnish with pistachios and serve.

Date Rolls (Ma'aroud)

Preparation time: 10 minutes
Cook time: 35 minutes
Nutrition facts (per serving): 203 cal (7g fat, 3g protein, 1g fiber)

The date rolls are great to serve with all the hot beverages, and they're popular for their prominent sweet and earthy taste.

Ingredients (8 servings)
Dough
4½ cups white flour
2 cups semolina flour
1 teaspoon baking powder
4 tablespoon sugar
13 ounces vegan butter
1 cup canola oil
1 ½ cups lukewarm water
1 teaspoon rose water

Filling
2 pounds soft dates, pitted
1 tablespoon canola oil
½ cup Concord wine
2 teaspoon cinnamon
Powdered sugar for decoration

Preparation

Mix white flour, semolina flour, baking powder, and sugar in a large bowl. Stir in vegan butter, canola oil, water, and rosewater. Combine well until it makes smooth dough. Soak the dates in warm water for 30 minutes, then peel and remove the pits. Dice the dates into small pieces and mix the dates with canola oil, wine, and cinnamon, then mix well. Divide the prepared dough into 8 equal-sized pieces and roll them into ½ cm thick rectangles. Split the dates filling on top of the rectangles. Roll the prepared dough rectangles and place them on a baking sheet. Bake for almost 35 minutes at 350 degrees F. Dust the rolls with sugar and serve.

Chocolate Halva Rugelach

Preparation time: 10 minutes
Cook time: 25 minutes
Nutrition facts (per serving): 58 cal (1.4g fat, 1g protein, 2g fiber)

These Israeli chocolate rugelaches are worth the try as they taste so unique and exotic. This dessert is definitely a must on the Israeli menu.

Ingredients (6 servings)
Dough
½ cup of sugar

⅛ teaspoon salt

2 cups all-purpose flour

2 sticks butter, cut into chunks

8 ounces cream cheese

⅓ cup sour cream

2 teaspoons vanilla

Filling
1 cup tahini paste

¼ teaspoon salt

6 tablespoons unsweetened cocoa powder

½ cup powdered sugar

Milk as needed

8 ounces chocolate, chopped

1 egg for egg wash

Sesame seeds

Preparation

Mix flour, salt and sugar in a bowl. Stir in cream cheese and cold butter, and then blend until crumbly. Add vanilla and sour cream, and then mix well for 1 minute until it makes smooth dough. Divide this dough into 4 equal-sized balls. Prepare the filling and mix sugar, cocoa powder, and tahini paste in a bowl. Stir milk and mix well. Spread each dough ball into 9 inches round circle. Divide the filling on top of each dough sheet and spread it evenly. Place ¼th chocolate pieces on top of each. Cut the rounds into triangles and roll each triangle. Place the chocolate rolls on a baking sheet and bake for 25 minutes. Serve.

Marble Halva

Preparation time: 15 minutes
Cook time: 10 minutes
Nutrition facts (per serving): 289 cal (13g fat, 3g protein, 2g fiber)

If you haven't tried this marble halva before, then here comes a simple and easy to cook recipe that you can recreate at home in no time with minimum efforts.

Ingredients (6 servings)
1-pound granulated sugar
1 pinch salt
4 ounces cold water
1-pound sesame tahini
1 teaspoon vanilla extract
5 ounces dark chocolate, melted

Preparation
Mix water, salt, and sugar in a saucepan over medium heat and boil until sugar is dissolved. Cook until the mixture thickens. Stir in the tahini and vanilla and then mix well. Pour this mixture into a baking pan and slowly pour the melted chocolate into the pan. Make swirls in the halva using a fork. Allow the halva to cool. Slice and serve.

Israeli Stuffed Dates

Preparation time: 15 minutes
Cook time: 1 minute
Nutrition facts (per serving): 86 cal (4g fat, 1g protein, 0g fiber)

The famous stuffed dates with chocolate and coconut on top are essential to try on the Israeli dessert menu. Try to prepare them at home with these basic ingredients and enjoy.

Ingredients (25 servings)

8 ounces bittersweet chocolate, chopped

25 pitted Medjool dates

25 pecan halves

2 tablespoons shredded coconut

Preparation

Melt chocolate in a bowl by heating it in the microwave for 30 seconds. Layer a baking sheet with aluminum foil. Stuff each date with pecans and place them on the baking sheet. Drizzle chocolate on top and sprinkle with coconut. Freeze the dates for 1 hour. Serve.

Israeli Chocolate Bites (Kadurei Shokolad)

Preparation time: 15 minutes
Nutrition facts (per serving): 228 cal (6g fat, 4g protein, 3g fiber)

These chocolate bites are one good option to go for in the desserts. You can also keep them ready and stored, and then serve them as an instant dessert.

Ingredients (8 servings)

1 sleeve petit beurre biscuits
1 stick butter, melted
⅓ cup of cocoa powder
½ cup of sugar
⅓ cup milk
1 teaspoon vanilla extract
1 ½ tablespoons brandy
¾ cup flaked coconut, coating
½ cup nonpareil candies, coating

Preparation

Crush the beurre biscuits in a food processor and mix well them well with melted butter, sugar, vanilla extract, cocoa powder, and milk in a bowl. Cover and refrigerate the mixture for 1 hour. Spread the coconut flakes on a plate. Divide the chocolate batter into bite-sized balls. Roll these balls into the coconut shreds. Drizzle the candies over the bites and serve.

Sweet Cheese Kanafeh

Preparation time: 10 minutes

Cook time: 20 minutes

Nutrition facts (per serving): 186 cal (12g fat, 4g protein, 2.5g fiber)

Without this sweet cheese kanafeh, it seems like the Israeli dessert menu is incomplete. Try them with different variations of toppings.

Ingredients (6 servings)

Syrup

1 cup of water

1 cup of sugar

1 cardamom pod

1 cinnamon stick

½ lemon, cut in half

½ orange, cut in half

Kadayif

1-pound kadayif noodles

12 ounces sweet goat cheese

8 tablespoons clarified butter

Garnish

1 cup ground pistachio

Preparation

Mix the lemon, orange, cinnamon stick, cardamom, sugar, and water in a saucepan and cook until the mixture is reduced to half. Strain and keep this syrup aside. Mix the kadayif noodles with butter in a skillet and drizzle cheese on top. Cover the noodles in the skillet and cook for 10 minutes on low heat. Remove the noodles from the heat and flip the kanafeh and cook for 3 minutes until golden. Pour the prepared syrup on top and garnish with pistachio. Serve.

Israeli Halvah

Preparation time: 10 minutes
Cook time: 8 minutes
Nutrition facts (per serving): 241 cal (4g fat, 2g protein, 1.1g fiber)

Here comes a dessert that's most loved by all. The Israeli halvah is not only served as a dessert, but it's also famous street food.

Ingredients (12 servings)
2 cups honey
1 ½ cups tahini
2 cups toasted almonds, sliced

Preparation
Add honey to a saucepan pan and cook until it reaches 240 degrees F. Stir in tahini and mix well until smooth. Fold in the nuts and then stir the mixture for 8 minutes. Pour the mixture into a baking pan and allow it to cool. Cut it into squares. Serve.

Israeli Fruit Salad

Preparation time: 10 minutes
Nutrition facts (per serving): 127 cal (11g fat, 1g protein, 2.1g fiber)

This fruit salad is the best salad to find in Israeli cuisine. This salad is so loaded with nutrients as it's prepared with figs, plums, and ripe pears.

Ingredients (4 servings)
2 ripe plums, unpeeled and sliced
2 red or green ripe pears, unpeeled and cubed
½ cup dates, pitted and chopped
½ cup fresh figs stemmed and sliced
½ cup pomegranate seeds
Zest and juice from 1 lime
¼ cup mint, chopped
1 tablespoon honey

Preparation
Toss all the fruit salad ingredients together in a salad bowl. Serve.

Drinks

Pomegranate Arak Mojito

Preparation time: 5 minutes
Nutrition facts (per serving): 112 cal (2g fat, 4 protein, 3g fiber)

Beat the heat and try the famous Israeli Arak mojito with the hints of lemon and pomegranate juice. The combination is super refreshing and healthy.

Ingredients (4 servings)

8 ounces mint leaves
½ cup honey
1 ½ cups of arak
1 cup pomegranate juice
1 ¼ cups citrus juice
1 cup of sparkling water
Ice as needed
2 cups of pomegranate arils
Citrus fruit slices

Preparation

Mash mint leaves with honey in a mortar with a pestle. Mix the mint mixture with arak, pomegranate juice, citrus juice, and ice in a cocktail shaker. Garnish with pomegranate arils and fruit slices. Serve.

Dead Sea Mule

Preparation time: 5 minutes
Nutrition facts (per serving): 103cal (7g fat, 3g protein, 1g fiber)

The Israeli Dead Sea mule is loved by all due to its refreshing taste and sweet flavors. Serve it chilled for the best taste and flavor.

Ingredients (2 servings)

2 ounces legal mezcal
¾ ounces Fresh lime juice
1-ounce Grenadine
5 ounces Fever-Tree ginger beer
Mint sprig, to garnish
Candied ginger, to garnish

Preparation

Mix grenadine with lime juice and mezcal in a Collins glass. Add ice and ginger beer and then garnish with a mint sprig. Thread the candied ginger on 2 small skewers. Garnish with the candied ginger. Serve

Israeli Cardamom Coffee

Preparation time: 10 minutes
Cook time: 5 minutes
Nutrition facts (per serving): 30 cal (0g fat, 0g protein, 5g fiber)

The Israeli cardamom coffee is great to serve on all special occasions and dinner, especially during the winter holidays.

Ingredients (2 servings)
8 ounces of water
5 teaspoons ground coffee
4 cardamom pods, grounded
2 dashes cinnamon
1 dash grated ginger
Sugar

Preparation
Mix water, sugar, ginger, cardamom, cinnamon, and coffee in a saucepan and cook until it boils. Serve warm.

Vive Shake

Preparation time: 10 minutes
Nutrition facts (per serving): 667 cal (34g fat, 24g protein, 1.5g fiber)

The tempting shake is made from a nice blend of yogurt with peach and orange juice. It has a crunchy texture due to the use of almond and granola.

Ingredients (1 serving)

1 (6 ounces) tub vanilla yogurt

6 frozen peach slices

3 ounces of orange juice

6 tablespoons slivered almonds

6 tablespoons granola

Preparation

Blend yogurt with peach slices, almonds, granola, and orange juice in a blender until smooth. Serve.

Coconut Milk Sachlav

Preparation time: 10 minutes
Cook time: 10 minutes
Nutrition facts (per serving): 142 cal (3g fat, 6.3g protein, 1g fiber)

The Israeli vegan Sachlav ul is famous for its blend of coconut milk with cinnamon and nuts. You can prepare this drink easily at home.

Ingredients (2 servings)

1 can full-fat coconut milk
1 teaspoon Ceylon cinnamon
2 teaspoons arrowroot powder
1 tablespoon coconut sugar

Toppings

Almonds
Walnuts
Cinnamon
Coconut Shreds
Pistachios

Preparation

Mix coconut milk with coconut sugar in a saucepan and boil, and then reduce the heat. Cook this mixture until it thickens. Stir in the arrowroot powder and cinnamon before mixing well. Garnish with almonds, walnuts, cinnamon, coconut shreds, and pistachios. Serve.

Sachlav

Preparation time: 5 minutes
Cook time: 3 minutes
Nutrition facts (per serving): 156 cal (0g fat, 0.7g protein, 1.4g fiber)

The Sachlav is all that you need to celebrate the holidays. Keep the drink ready in your refrigerator for quick serving.

Ingredients (4 serving)
3 cups almond milk
1 tablespoon sugar
2 teaspoons vanilla extract
2 tablespoons rice flour
½ teaspoon rose water
Pinch of sea salt

Topping
Shredded coconut
Ground cinnamon
Chopped pistachios
Chopped walnuts

Preparation
Mix the almond milk with sea salt, rose water, rice flour, vanilla beans, and sugar in a suitable saucepan and cook over low heat for 3 minutes. Divide the mixture into cups and garnish with coconut, cinnamon, pistachios, and walnuts. Serve.

Lemon Mix

Preparation time: 5 minutes

Nutrition facts (per serving): 131 cal (11g fat, 10g protein, 0.3g fiber)

It's a special Israeli drink made out of tubi 60 spirit, which is lovely to serve at special dinners and celebrations.

Ingredients (2 servings)

2 ounces Tubi 60 spirit

4 ounces Schweppes bitter lemon

3 pieces lemon

1-piece mint

5 pieces of ice

Preparation

Add Tubi, bitter lemon, lemon, mint, and ice to a cocktail shaker. Lastly, mix well. Serve.

Israeli Limonana

Preparation time: 5 minutes
Nutrition facts (per serving): 110 cal (0g fat, 0g protein, 2.3g fiber)

Here's a special Israeli Lemonade drink, which is great for digestion and beats the heat when served during scorching summers.

Ingredients (4 servings)

½ cup of sugar

1 ¾ cups water

1 cup fresh lemon juice

3 ½ cups ice

1 cup fresh mint leaves

5 mint sprigs for garnish

Preparation

Pour or add all the ingredients to a blender and blend for 60 seconds. Serve.

Sahlab

Preparation time: 5 minutes
Cook time: 2 minutes
Nutrition facts (per serving): 222 cal (14g fat, 7g protein, 0.8g fiber)

It's a lovely mix of milk, nuts, and sugar is all that you need to expand your Israeli menu. Simple and easy to make, this recipe is a must to try.

Ingredients (4 servings)
4 cups whole milk
3 ½ tablespoons cornstarch
6 teaspoons granulated sugar
1 teaspoon pure vanilla extract
½ teaspoon ground cinnamon
1 tablespoon desiccated coconut
¼ cup walnuts, chopped
2 tablespoons raisins

Preparation
Whisk the sugar, milk, vanilla, and cornstarch in a cooking pot and cook for 2 minutes. Pour into the serving glasses. Garnish with nuts, coconut, and cinnamon. Serve.

If you liked Israeli recipes, discover to how cook DELICIOUS recipes from **Balkan** countries!

Within these pages, you'll learn 35 authentic recipes from a Balkan cook. These aren't ordinary recipes you'd find on the Internet, but recipes that were closely guarded by our Balkan mothers and passed down from generation to generation.

Main Dishes, Appetizers, and Desserts included!

If you want to learn how to make Croatian green peas stew, and 32 other authentic Balkan recipes, then start with our book!

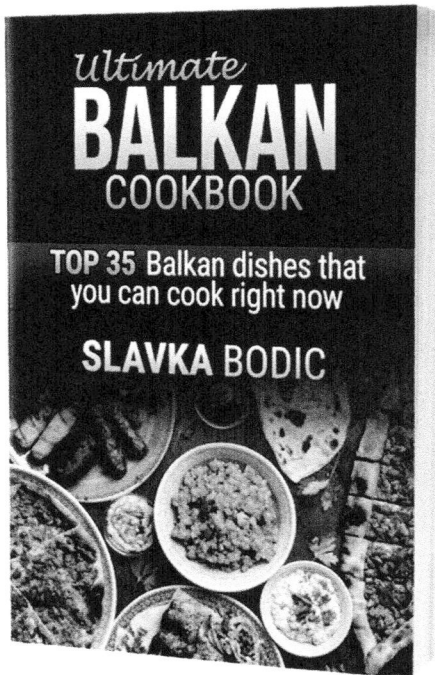

Order at www.balkanfood.org/cook-books/ for only $2,99

If you're a **Mediterranean** dieter who wants to know the secrets of the Mediterranean diet, dieting, and cooking, then you're about to discover how to master cooking meals on a Mediterranean diet right now!

In fact, if you want to know how to make Mediterranean food, then this new e-book - "The 30-minute Mediterranean diet" - gives you the answers to many important questions and challenges every Mediterranean dieter faces, including:

- How can I succeed with a Mediterranean diet?
- What kind of recipes can I make?
- What are the key principles to this type of diet?
- What are the suggested weekly menus for this diet?
- Are there any cheat items I can make?

... and more!

If you're serious about cooking meals on a Mediterranean diet and you really want to know how to make Mediterranean food, then you need to grab a copy of "The 30-minute Mediterranean diet" right now.

Prepare **111 recipes with several ingredients in less than 30 minutes**!

Order at www.balkanfood.org/cook-books/ for only $2,99

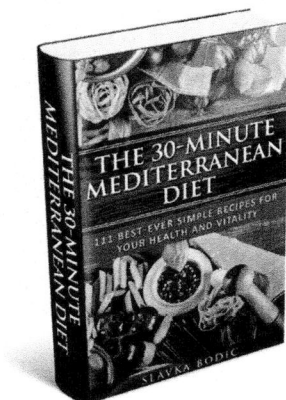

What could be better than a home-cooked meal? Maybe only a **Greek** homemade meal.

Do not get discouraged if you have no Greek roots or friends. Now you can make a Greek food feast in your kitchen.

This ultimate Greek cookbook offers you 111 best dishes of this cuisine! From more famous gyros to more exotic *Kota Kapama* this cookbook keeps it easy and affordable.

All the ingredients necessary are wholesome and widely accessible. The author's picks are as flavorful as they are healthy. The dishes described in this cookbook are "what Greek mothers have made for decades."

Full of well-balanced and nutritious meals, this handy cookbook includes many vegan options. Discover a plethora of benefits of Mediterranean cuisine, and you may fall in love with cooking at home.

Inspired by a real food lover, this collection of delicious recipes will taste buds utterly satisfied.

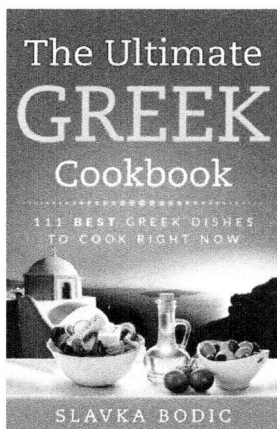

Order at www.balkanfood.org/cook-books/ for only $2,99

Maybe to try exotic **Syrian** cuisine?

From succulent *sarma*, soups, warm and cold salads to delectable desserts, the plethora of flavors will satisfy the most jaded foodie. Have a taste of a new culture with this **traditional Syrian cookbook**.

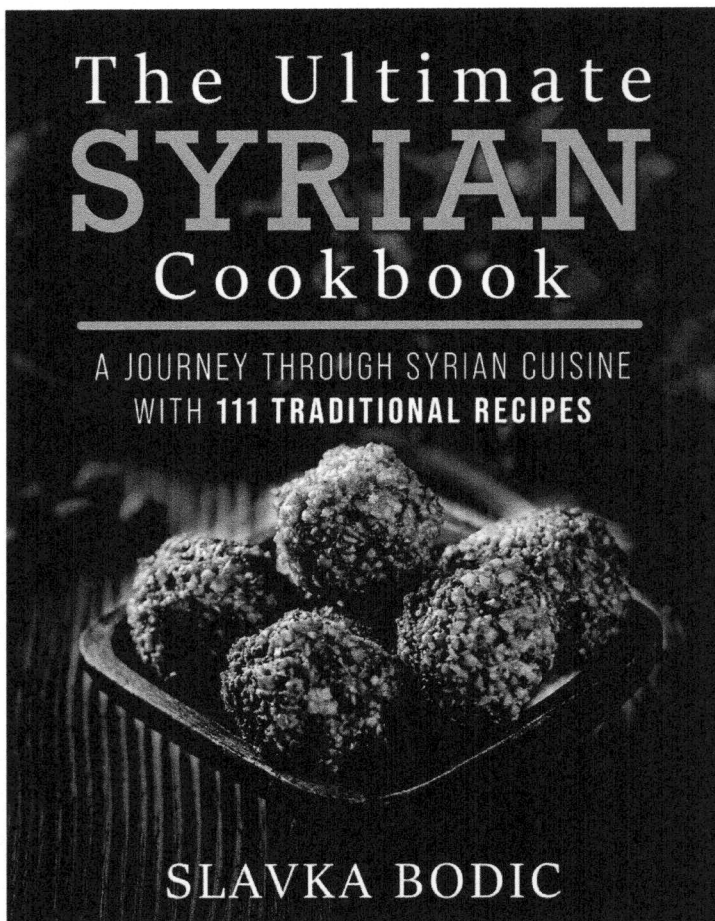

Order at www.balkanfood.org/cook-books/ for only $2,99

Maybe **Polish** or **Korean** cuisine?

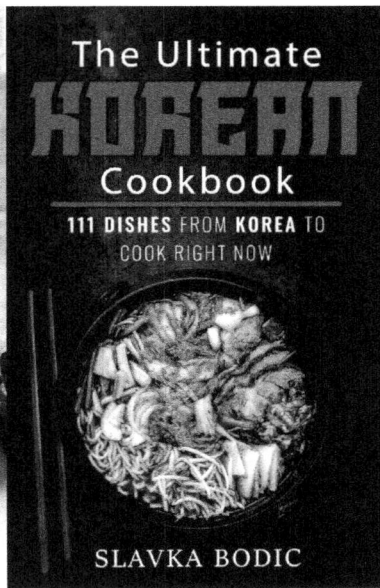

Order at www.balkanfood.org/cook-books/ for only $2,99

Or **Peruvian?**

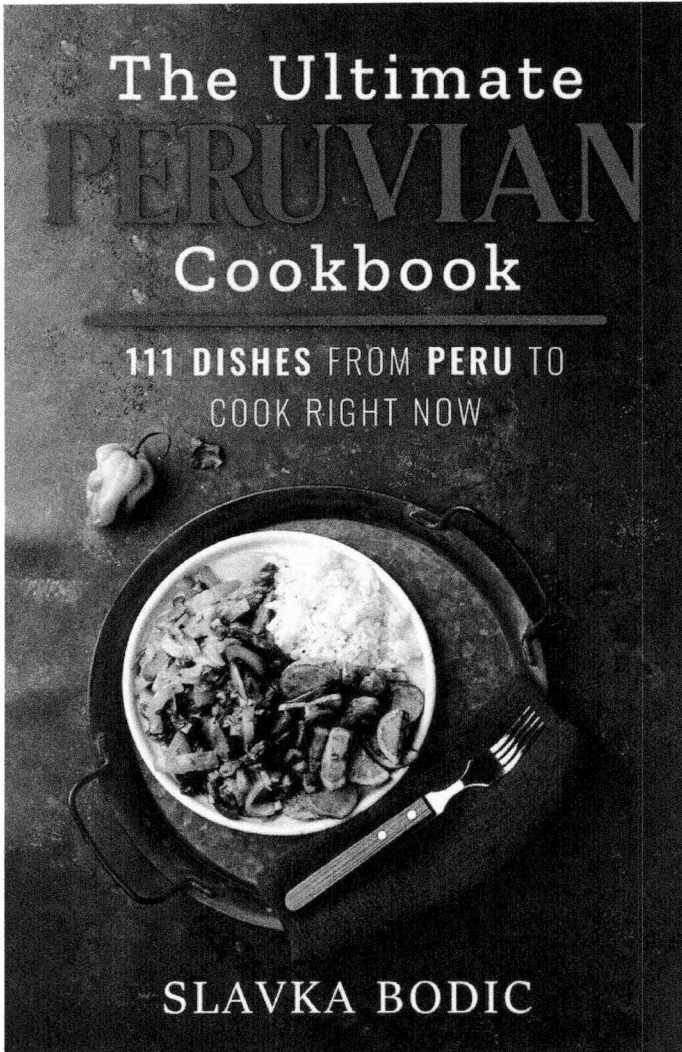
Order at www.balkanfood.org/cook-books/ for only $2,99

ONE LAST THING

If you enjoyed this book or found it useful, I'd be very grateful if you could find the time to post a short review on Amazon. Your support really does make a difference and I read all the reviews personally, so I can get your feedback and make this book even better.

Thanks again for your support!

Please send me your feedback at

www.balkanfood.org

Printed in Great Britain
by Amazon